Animals are SMARTER than JACK

91 amazing true animal stories

Connecting animal lovers and helping animals worldwide

The publisher
Smarter than Jack Limited (a subsidiary of Avocado Press Limited)
Australia: PO Box 170, Ferntree Gully, Victoria, 3156
Canada: PO Box 819, Tottenham, Ontario, L0G 1W0
New Zealand: PO Box 27003, Wellington
www.smarterthanjack.com

The creators
SMARTER than JACK series concept and creation: Jenny Campbell
Compiler and typesetting: Lisa Richardson
Administration: Anthea Kirk
Cover design: DNA Design, Simon Cosgrove and Lisa Richardson
Cover photograph: © Rachael Hale Photography (NZ) Ltd 2004. All rights reserved.
Rachael Hale is a registered trademark of Rachael Hale Photography Limited.
Illustrations: Arja Hone
Story typing and editing: Patricia Reesby
Story selection: Jenny Campbell, Lisa Richardson, Anthea Kirk, Lydia Crysell and others
Proofreading: Vicki Andrews (Animal Welfare in Print)
North American office: Eric Adriaans

The book trade distributors
Australia: Bookwise International
Canada: Publishers Group Canada
New Zealand: Addenda Publishing
United Kingdom: Airlift Book Company
United States: Publishers Group West

The legal details
First published 2005
ISBN 0-9582571-8-3

Contents

Responsible animal care iv
Creating your SMARTER than JACK. v
Connecting animal lovers worldwide. vi
The enchanting cover photo vii
The delightful illustrations. viii
1 Smart animals take control 1
2 Smart animals prevent disasters 15
3 Smart animals learn fast. 29
4 Smart animals to the rescue 39
5 Smart animals get revenge and outwit us 57
6 Smart animals find solutions 69
Your say 82
7 Smart animals have fun 85
8 Smart animals make us wonder 97
9 Smart animals teach us lessons 117
The SMARTER than JACK story 141
Submit a story for our books. 143
Receive a free SMARTER than JACK gift pack. 145
Get more wonderful stories 147

Responsible animal care

The stories in this book have been carefully reviewed to ensure that they do not promote the mistreatment of animals in any way.

It is important to note, however, that animal care practices can vary substantially from country to country, and often depend on factors such as climate, population density, predators, disease control, local by-laws and social norms. Animal care practices can also change considerably over time; in some instances, practices considered perfectly acceptable many years ago are now considered unacceptable.

Therefore, some of the stories in this book may involve animals in situations that are not normally acceptable in your community. We strongly advise that you consult with your local animal welfare charity if you are in any way unsure about the best way to care for animals in your community.

You may also find, when reading these stories, that you can learn from other people's (often unfortunate) mistakes. For example, if you have a dog it is important to make sure that it is appropriately and safely secured when you are not at home, and under close control in public places. Water can be a hazard too; if you have a swimming pool check that it is adequately fenced, and always keep your dog secure while at the marina! Cars are another potential danger; ideally you should not leave your dog alone in a car, but if this is unavoidable, make sure there is adequate ventilation and that it is only for a very short time.

We also advise that you take care to ensure your pet does not eat poisonous plants or other dangerous substances, and do not give any animal alcohol. In some rather extreme cases, you may even need to monitor what television channels your pet watches!

Creating your SMARTER than JACK

Animals are SMARTER than JACK is a heart-warming book of tales about truly smart animals.

Many talented and generous people have had a hand in the creation of this book. This includes everyone who submitted a story, and especially those who had a story selected as this provided the content for this inspiring book. The people who gave us constructive feedback on earlier books and cover design, and those who participated in our research, helped us make this book even better.

The people at the participating animal welfare charities assisted us greatly and were wonderful to work with. Profit from sales will help these animal welfare charities in their admirable quest to improve animal welfare.

Lisa Richardson compiled the stories, did the typesetting and helped with the cover design, Rachael Hale provided the beautiful cover photograph, Pat Reesby typed and edited stories, Anthea Kirk helped coordinate all the entries, Vicki Andrews did the proofreading, Arja Hone drew the lovely illustrations, Simon Cosgrove helped with the cover, and many others helped with the enormous task of selecting and typing the stories.

Thanks to bookstores for making this book widely available to our readers, and thanks to readers for purchasing this book and for enjoying it and for giving it to others as gifts.

Lastly, I cannot forget my endearing companion Ford the cat. Ford is now 12 years old and has been by my side all the way through the inspiring SMARTER than JACK journey.

We hope you enjoy **Animals are SMARTER than JACK** – and we hope that many animals and people benefit from it.

Jenny Campbell
Creator of SMARTER than JACK

Connecting animal lovers worldwide

Our readers and story contributors love to share their experiences and adventures with other like-minded people. So to help them along we've added a few new features to our books.

You can now write direct to many of the contributors about your experiences with the animals in your life. Some contributors have included their contact details with their story. If an email address is given and you don't have access to the internet, just write a letter and send it via us and we'll be happy to send it on.

We also welcome your letters for our 'Your say' section. These could be about animals in your life or about people who are out there making a difference.

Do you have an unusual question that other readers may be able to help answer? Some readers have posed a number of interesting questions, scattered throughout this book. Can you answer them?

Do you like to write to friends and family by mail? In the back of this book we've included some special SMARTER than JACK story postcards. Why not keep in touch and spread the smart animal word at the same time.

Since 2002 the popular SMARTER than JACK series has helped raise over NZ$280,000 for animal welfare charities. It is now helping animals in Canada, the United States, Australia, New Zealand and the United Kingdom.

The future of the SMARTER than JACK series holds a number of exciting books – there will be ones about cheeky animals, heroic animals and intuitive animals. You can subscribe to the series now too; more information can be found in the back of this book.

If you've had an amazing encounter with a smart animal we'd love to read about it. You may also like to sign up to receive the Story of the Week for a bit of inspiration – visit www.smarterthanjack.com

The enchanting cover photo

Masquerading behind the adoring expressions of our much loved pets are the stories and adventures, capers and escapades that have endeared them to our hearts and made them all a special part of the family.

This wonderful new edition of stories about everyday animals is brought to life with the enchanting cover photograph by renowned photographer Rachael Hale. Her distinctive images, famous around the world, capture the character and personality of her favorite friends, while allowing her to continue to support her favorite charity, the SPCA.

With the success of this series of animal anecdotes now established in New Zealand, Australia, Canada and soon the United Kingdom and United States, perhaps the best story is that the sale of every book makes a generous contribution to animal welfare in that country.

Rachael Hale Photography is proud to be associated with the SMARTER than JACK book series and trusts you'll enjoy these heart-warming stories that create such cherished images of our pets, along with the delightful pictures that tell such wonderful stories themselves.

David Todd
Rachael Hale Photography Limited
www.rachaelhale.com

The delightful illustrations

The series of illustrations at the bottom of each page are the work of Arja Hone. Arja lives in Wellington, New Zealand with her husband Chris, and together they are owned by a cat called Penny.

Arja secretly hopes that reincarnation theories are true, and that she has been good enough in this life to come back as a house cat.

Arja can be contacted by email at ajris@paradise.net.nz.

1

Smart animals take control

Fair exchange?

While I was preparing for a garage sale a neighbor dropped in with a carton of cuddly toys. Susie, my ten-year-old silky terrier, gave the toys a quick inspection. She decided on a white teddy bear almost as big as herself, took it by the arm, gently removed it from the box and placed it on her favorite mat. Susie then picked up her small, much worse for wear rag-dog, and placed it in the box.

Daphne Maconachie
Atherton, Queensland
Australia

Minnie and Mickey look out for one another

My parents have two cats called Minnie and Mickey (brother and sister) who are two years old. They are very close and look out for one another.

Mickey likes to go up on the roof of the house and relax in the sun, but when it's time to come down he needs help. This is where his sister comes in.

Minnie will go and find my dad. If he is outside she will meow and meow, and if he is inside she will bat her paws at the door almost like she is trying to knock. Once she has his attention she

leads the way and Dad will follow. Then she will stop, look up and start meowing. At this point, Mickey will start meowing too. Dad will look up, and who is lying on the edge of the roof wanting to get down? Mickey.

Dad gets the ladder, goes up and gets Mickey, and the cats go off and play together. This is a regular routine for Mickey and Minnie – they do everything together. They are wonderful pets and companions for my parents, who are seniors. Mickey and Minnie are very lucky to have owners like Mom and Dad who love and spoil them as much as they do.

Ursula Schetterer
Calgary, Alberta
Canada

Write to me ...
Ursula Schetterer
225-215-86 Ave SE
Calgary AB T2H 2K5
CANADA

One helpful goat

We share our long driveway with our neighbors. They decided to get a goat to help keep the driveway grass down, and so Steve (named after Steve Irwin) arrived.

He is a lovely animal who is also so considerate at getting up and moving away whenever a car comes down the driveway. He has a hut and a bucket of water that is moved with him up and down the driveway, and sometimes he even gets an extra bucketful of goat goodies.

One morning as my husband Frank was on his way to work in the ute he saw Steve sitting in the middle of the drive next to his bucket of yummy treats. Frank was thinking he would have to stop and get out to move the bucket as he wouldn't be able to maneuver past.

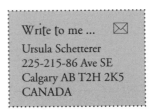

Steve was also summing up the situation as he looked first at the ute, then back at the bucket, then back at the ute, then back at the bucket. He must have been coming to the same conclusion as Frank because, to my husband's amazement, Steve picked up the bucket and moved it over to the side.

Frank couldn't help but chuckle to himself as he drove past, but what really got him laughing was when he looked in the rear-view mirror to see Steve walking out to the middle of the drive with the bucket. As Frank watched, Steve put the bucket down in just the same spot as before.

Julie Aerts
Tokoroa
New Zealand

The bantam baby-snatcher

The Little Brown One, as she is known, is the most perfect mother you could imagine.

Our bantam hen instructs her offspring in the survival stakes, and makes sure they don't eat until she has inspected the goodies we've put in the chook bucket. The chicks do escape from her on rare occasions, but always run back to hide under her wings.

All this, and she has never laid an egg.

To satisfy her broodiness and become a mother herself, she muscles in on another hen. The chosen hen is always sitting on eggs that are about a week away from hatching. It seems the two hens take turns at egg sitting, and there are a few scraps between them.

When the eggs start to hatch, the takeover starts in earnest. The Brown One pushes the real mother repeatedly out of the cubicle, and within a day or two the takeover is complete. The chicks' real

mum returns to wandering around with the harem, while the Brown One begins her task of bringing up yet another acquired brood. Heaven help any hen that goes near the chicks, including their own mother.

We conned her into bringing up three little Rhode Island Red chicks by sneaking the eggs into the nest along with those already there. She seems such a docile wee thing … until she decides she wants a family.

June Spragg
Ahuroa, Warkworth
New Zealand

When The Little Brown One wants a family, she simply takes one

Tonia's trip to the vet

I had a beautiful big black Newfoundland called Tonia. We had a ritual for our daily walk: when we got to the gate, Tonia would choose which way we would go. She knew the routes well enough after all those years to know what going to the right as opposed to the left would offer.

This particular day she chose to go left. She didn't choose this way very often because it was a shorter walk. I hesitated, but she pulled me quite firmly in that direction as only a 58 kilogram dog could! There was real purpose in her stride this day. Usually she ambled along at her own pace because now she was getting old.

We got to the end of the street, turned left and headed up to the main road. Tonia usually turned right there. We rarely walked this way because of all the traffic. It meant we had to wait for a break in it and dash across the road because there were no traffic lights or crossing. I was becoming more curious by the minute as I let her lead the way.

We approached the roundabout and negotiated the traffic there, crossing safely. Instead of heading to the walking track, we continued along the main road. Then it clicked. This was the way we walked to the vet sometimes. Surely she wasn't taking me there! Tonia was no different from most animals, she didn't particularly like going to the vet. Why would she head this way if that wasn't the reason?

We approached the driveway we used to cross the road to the vet. This was the moment of truth. Sure enough, she went down it and sat waiting for the traffic to clear before we crossed. Tonia trotted quite purposefully through the automatic glass doors, parked her bottom right in front of the reception desk, tongue lolling, and looked up at me expectantly.

The receptionist greeted us, assuming we had an appointment. My jaw had dropped by now and I was speechless. Gathering my

wits, I explained the story to her. I asked if we could see a vet since Tonia had gone to all the trouble of bringing herself there. I was expecting a long wait because we hadn't made an appointment.

Just then, the vet we usually saw poked his head out of the consulting room and said hello. Still in a state of amazement I told him the story. As it happened, he was free and could see her right away. On examining her, he discovered she had a urinary tract infection that required treatment! Tonia must have had enough of the discomfort from the infection, so had taken action as I obviously hadn't picked up that she was unwell.

On the way home she reverted to her usual ambling pace, and I held a white paper bag containing her antibiotics. I couldn't wait to get back to tell my husband the story. He was as amazed as the receptionist, the vet and I were. Who says animals aren't smart!

Julie Biro
Mt Evelyn, Victoria
Australia

Write to me ...
Julie Biro
PO Box 279
Mt Evelyn VIC 3796
AUSTRALIA

Why won't they let us in?

When we sold our house a few years ago, the usual real estate agent wagon train came through for an inspection.

My husband and I were both at work, and the house was empty except for Henri, our not-so-shy parrot. Of course, the agents knocked at the door before entering and through the closed front door they heard a very loud voice calling *Hello*.

The agents stood back and waited to be let in. They waited and waited but no one opened the door. Again they knocked. By now, the queue of agents was growing, all of them with that ever hopeful look of '*When* is the door to be opened?' Henri kept repeating *Hello, Hello*.

As time went on, a brave agent made the decision to unlock the door. Of course, he was met by an overexcited Henri jumping up and down on his perch. The agents were so amused that our fully stocked lolly jar was reduced by half as they chatted away to our parrot. Hopefully, his usual choice of language (not taught by us) didn't slip out and lower the selling price.

Rob Vukich
Howick, Auckland
New Zealand

Marmalade goes walking by herself

I knew what I would call her before I even met her. Marmalade is an apt name for a pot-bellied pig, don't you think?

I love pigs and really wanted a regular pink farm animal, but whenever I broached the subject my partner balked. One glorious winter day, Marmalade came into my life. She and her nine siblings, about six months old, had been dropped off in an alley behind a seedy hotel on Skid Row in Vancouver.

A biker living in the hotel picked her up and kept her in his room for a couple of days. He gave her to an 'animal angel' who rescues all sorts of creatures. Marmalade was placed in a cat carrier and flown over to Gabriola Island from Vancouver in a seaplane. I picked her up at Silva Bay, drove her home and introduced her to the family. She sleeps under a blanket on her bed beside our wood cooking stove in the kitchen. When she was little she slept under the stove alongside one of our cats, but now her head barely fits underneath.

Marmalade's walks can take up to two and a half hours

I started taking her for walks down our long driveway and down to a main road. We'd turn around and go home, with the promise of a banana halfway. We live on a dead-end road so traffic is light.

It took a while for her to get used to the noise of a vehicle. At first I used a dog harness, and then bought an expensive hot-pink pot-bellied pig harness. With everything I tried, she ended up with sores so I gave up. I can't make her do anything she doesn't want to do, anyway.

I walked her for three years, starting out twice a day and going for nearly a mile. It would take us about 45 minutes. As time went on, the walks got longer but the distance got shorter, so I cut the walks down to once a day. Then the time got longer and longer, until it was taking one and a half hours to go for a walk. You see, Marmalade likes to 'visit' with anyone on the road, or hang out and do a little rooting.

Finally, I'd had enough of waiting for her so I told her she could go for walks by herself. The first day, she waited two hours for me to come and I felt mean. She finally gave up waiting and left, complaining the whole time. Today, she continues to walk by herself but if the weather is inclement she complains, at least until I'm out of earshot. She wears a ribbon (soft surveyor's tape that comes in bright pink, green and orange), with her name, phone number and the words 'I take walks by myself' on it.

She spends up to two and a half hours on the road, depending on the weather and the friends she meets. When I used to walk with her, I often had to stop her from going into driveways. On her own she rarely enters driveways – unless, of course, she sees a particular friend who cuts up an apple for her.

Sharon Marshall
Gabriola Island, British Columbia
Canada

Marvelous Martin

Long ago in the late '60s and in a place far away (California), my young bride and I became the parents of a kitten that we named Martin Luther Cat. Since we were about to go on our honeymoon, we had to train him to come to my whistling.

We intended to travel from California to Florida in a camper with Martin as company. Each time we made a rest stop or camped for the night, we trusted that Martin would return when I whistled. Sure enough, over our circuitous route from California through Illinois down to Florida and then back, Martin stayed with us. As I have since found out, cats think that people are their family and, if you feed them, they bond with you as the papa cat and mama cat.

Alone, camping by lakes and streams, we spent a lot of time petting our cat and talking to him. Martin was good company and

very loyal, so when we returned to California and found a new home he settled right in. He always watched everything we did and, like all observant cats, followed our routines. He knew that we would hurry to the phone when it rang and we would go and open the door when someone knocked. He watched us and, of course, during his studies, he discovered everything about getting fed and where we kept his food.

Every weekday, my wife and I would go off to teach, leaving Martin at home. Having this empty apartment to himself must have been a big challenge for Martin. He must have felt responsible to carry on for us, since he took on answering the phone and opening the front door.

Coming home from school and finding the door open or the phone off the hook I dismissed as carelessness, until the day I phoned home and, after a few rings, the phone was answered and a meow was heard. I had to see this for myself so I went home and waited for my wife to call. She called and let the phone ring. After it went for quite a while, Martin came charging around a corner, jumped up on the hall table, stood on his rear paws, and using his front paws pushed the receiver off the hook. As if that feat wasn't enough, he put his nose to the mouthpiece and meowed.

So there it was – the handset lying on the hall table and Martin meowing into it.

Seeing a cat on the phone was incredible, but he topped it one day when I didn't get to the front door in time and found him swinging with both paws clenched around the knob. The knob was the old style with a relief engraved into it for traction. Martin was able to hang on as he swung from side to side until the knob turned and the door opened.

Marvelous Martin was a stunner.

He traveled with us for the rest of his life, finally settling on our farm in Maui, Hawaii. He stopped answering phones and opening doors but, hearing the upstairs toilet flush, my wife and I just shook our heads and smiled, 'Oh, Marvelous Martin, you're at it again.'

Mike Ward
Mangonui
New Zealand

Write to me ...
email Mike
mikaeleward@yahoo.com

Hurry up, I'm getting impatient

Years ago I adopted a poodle mix named Baboo from the local Humane Society.

One day I took him in the car with me and went into a store. I could hear a horn honking but didn't pay any attention to it. When I came out there were people standing around my car watching as Baboo blew the horn, then waited to see if I was coming or not. He did this right up to the year he died.

Lesa Donnelly
Prince Edward Island
Canada

Donna knew what to do … and did it!

Donna, a five-year-old Rottweiler, almost cost me my job.

I used to take her on my night shifts in a factory I worked in about 15 years ago, and together we passed the hours between 11 pm and 6 am. The factory was on automatic during this time, and the siren alarm system was supposed to alert the sole charge attendant (me) to any problems.

One night I fell asleep. Okay, that happened a lot, but this time the story got complicated.

Donna knew the drill. When the alarms went off, I got up off my seat/couch/bed and walked/ran out to the factory floor, switched off the alarm system causing the problem (indicated by the blinking red light) and fixed it. She had seen it countless times.

The first I knew I was caught out was when the relief shift at 6 am woke me up.

'Why is machine 3 on half power and the alarms switched off?' he said as he shook me awake. '*Whhhhhaaattt?*' I responded as I came to. Sure enough, the machine was producing only half its normal output, and the alarm system was shut down. A creepy, tingly feeling shot up my spine. That machine was okay, with the alarms switched on, when I checked the plant at midnight before bedding down for the night. It may not have been a course of action the boss would have been happy with, but everyone did it. The doors were locked and I was alone. It was a story out of the twilight zone. How did it happen?

I begged my relief to keep quiet about the incident, and during the next few days I searched the building for ways my workmates might have pulled a prank on me. It was about a week later that I figured out what must have happened. I decided to find out for certain.

I took Donna with me to the factory on a shift when my relief of that previous night was on watch. I tripped the alarm on machine 3 and hid in the office where I could watch. The alarm siren sounded and Donna started to grumble in her sleep from the corner of the factory staffroom. After five minutes she decided enough was enough and action was required.

She looked around for me, then trotted out onto the factory floor and located the winking light. She walked straight up to it and

When Tony fell asleep on the job, Donna took over

flipped the switch off with her nose. Satisfied with a job well done, she returned to her warm spot on the carpet – while my colleague and I watched in disbelief.

Why she chose to sort it out herself rather than wake me up and why the siren failed to stir me I have never figured out, but I was very nervous about sleeping on night shift after that. If only I could teach her to actually fix the problem as well as shut off the alarms …

Donna sadly is no longer with us, but I have never met a dog with as much intelligence as that one. I still miss her.

Tony Southern
Wellington
New Zealand

How can I reduce Charlie's caffeine dependency?

I have a horse called Charlie. Over the last couple of years I have been quite naughty and have been giving him coffee. Charlie just loves it and if I don't bring him his daily cup – with two sugars – he stamps his feet and refuses to be caught.

I spoke to my 'horsey friend' about this recently and she said that coffee was not good for horses and that under no circumstances should he have it. What should I do?

Can you offer any advice? Contact us at SMARTER than JACK.

2

Smart animals prevent disasters

I thought you meant it

My mom bought me a husky cross for Christmas. I named her Snowball as she was a big white ball of fur.

When she was about three years old we took her camping with us. The only reason she came was because I told my mom that if she couldn't go I wasn't going either.

It was late at night and we were getting ready to go to bed when Mom started stamping on the fire with her rubber boots on. She shouted for help, but was just pretending.

Snowball heard her shouting and ran over to her. She jumped up, knocking her to the ground and out of harm's way. Then she jumped on the fire and started pounding it with her paws.

A Picco
Newfoundland
Canada

The mockingbird's own true voice

The mockingbird can sing the songs of as many as 40 other birds.

I've heard a mockingbird mimic the trill of a purple martin so well that I thought the martins had arrived in the middle of winter. But, for all their amazing imitations, the mockingbird's true voice is a scratchy rasp, which you'll hear when they are angry or agitated. It is this voice that I have come to love, thanks to one ingenious mockingbird.

We lived on a little spot of land on the rolling coastal plains of south central Texas, where snakes are as common as prickly pear. We were sitting under a huge old live oak late one afternoon, when a mockingbird landed on the fence just beyond the yard, making tons of racket in her scratchy voice. I didn't know what she was upset about. One beer later she was still jumping around on the fence and swooping into the low branches above us, squawking and carrying on.

Finally she flew over to the sandy edge of the garden, less than ten feet from where we sat. She began to hop on the ground in a perfect circle, round and round again, all the while screeching and scratching her song of urgency. I stood up and went toward her, and realized she was circling a snake that had shimmied its way right toward us. It was in her own true voice that she alerted us to danger.

Maybe she had a nest in the tree above and was soliciting help to protect it. Sometimes I think back and imagine she was protecting us. But I have never stopped pondering the paradox of the mockingbird's voice. It is the true voice that comes when there is something important to be said.

Debbie Ventura
Pleasanton, Texas
United States

Just like Lassie

Nelson, our beautiful beagle dog, was as devoted to us as we were to him.

One night, about two years ago, a sudden powerful storm hit the eastern suburbs of Melbourne. Suddenly, the ceiling in our wardrobe began to balloon and fill with water. Wasting no time, my husband climbed up onto the steel deck roof at the front of our house to unclog the drain, which was causing the water to gush into the roof. He cleared the blockage and then stood up, silhouetted against the backdrop of the constant lightning, and called to me that he had cleared the drain. I could see he was feeling very proud of himself that he had saved all our clothes from a disaster.

Unfortunately, he wasn't able to enjoy his moment of glory for very long. The roof was dangerously wet and, as the rain cascaded onto it, the roof had become like a slippery dip. In one split second, he slipped off the roof and onto the brick path below.

I was terrified. My husband lay motionless in the pouring rain. I raced inside to phone for an ambulance. However, I must have screamed in fright, which alerted Nelson, who, unbeknown to me, came running out of the front door, which I had left open when I raced inside. He ran up to my husband lying on the ground, nuzzled him, then dashed off in the pouring rain for help.

Our neighbors told us later that they had heard a noise above the sound of the storm and had gone to their front door to look out. Their front door was in an adjacent street to ours and they could not see into our front garden. While they stood there wondering if they should go out to look around in the terrible conditions, Nelson appeared in the light from their front porch. They told us later he was just like Lassie in the movies. *Please come and help!* he seemed to be saying, and waited impatiently for them to follow him.

Nelson and the neighbors arrived to help at the accident scene. Then the ambulance arrived and my husband was taken to hospital. Our neighbors comforted our shaken daughter and followed the ambulance, with her in their car. They stayed with us all until, miraculously, my husband was told that he had only sustained minor injuries. His lucky star had been shining that night!

The true star of that evening had been our beautiful dog. We were amazed at Nelson's ability to size up the situation and realize that his mum and dad were in trouble. He was a dog who was never allowed out on his own and always walked on a lead. His best doggy friend, a dear little Maltese shih-tzu cross, lived next door and he had been to visit on several occasions, but only as a treat for the two dogs.

How had he known to leave the warmth of his comfy couch and run out into the cold and the rain to our wonderful neighbors for help? He was always treated as a member of our family and he certainly never regarded himself as a dog, but I believe it took a very high level of intelligence for him to embark on his specific search for help on that night.

Our family was so fortunate to have a happy ending to this accident. My husband came home nursing a couple of broken ribs and a very sore ankle, but he gave his wonderful dog the biggest hug he had ever had in his life.

Suzanne Coomes
Canterbury, Victoria
Australia

Write to me ...
email Suzanne
scoomes@hotmail.com

The little dog

Owen Farnham, with his wife and family, owned a farm at One Tree Point until about 35 years ago when they moved to a farm at Waiharara, north of Kaitaia. They sold the farm and it was developed for housing. Part of it is now known as Paradise Point.

Between then and now, Owen reached the age of 85 and, hale and hearty, he retired to Kaitaia, with his son Charlie taking over the farm.

For many years Owen has driven himself out to the farm to help out. He catches and saddles his horse, unclips his two dogs and, with his grubber across his shoulder, puts a few sandwiches and a thermos in his backpack and a few other essentials in his pocket. He then rides off to inspect the place, grub a few thistles and jot down in a notebook anything that might need doing, such as fence repairs.

On one particular day, he had ridden right out to Big Hill near the back of the farm and came to grief opening the gate while on his horse. The gate swung the wrong way and, in turning his horse to get the gate, the horse's rump touched the electric fence. The startled horse bolted, dislodging its passenger, who lay on the ground with a broken femur. The two dogs snuggled down beside him, while he pondered about a man he had heard of who had survived in a similar predicament for three days before he was found.

It was not long before the next-door neighbor's little dog arrived on the scene. This little dog was not a frequent visitor to the farm; in fact, Owen had never seen him out there before. He had a sudden thought that the little dog might go home to his owner, if Owen and the big dogs chased him off. First, Owen patted him and took out his notebook and wrote 'I am out by the gate to Big Hill and I can't walk, Owen'.

Owen always carried rubber bands around his notebook, so he tucked the note around a couple of rubber bands and stretched the

bands around the dog's neck. Owen then chased the little dog off, shouting, 'Get home, get away home.' The big dogs joined in with loud barks. The little dog went away – but he didn't go home.

Meanwhile, Charlie had arrived back at the farmhouse and his wife said, 'I'm a bit worried about your dad, he should be back by now.'

Charlie had just about set out to look for him when up trotted the little dog, tail wagging. When Charlie bent to pat him he noticed the note tucked in around the little dog's neck with rubber bands. He was so surprised to see the little dog, because he never visited by himself but sometimes came over with his owner, the next-door neighbor.

It wasn't long before Charlie and his wife were off in the four-wheel drive to find Owen back in the rough country. They brought him out carefully, phoning for the ambulance on the way via cellphone.

It didn't seem long before Owen was back on the horse again. He was amazed at what the little dog had done.

Joan Phillips
Ruakaka
New Zealand

Gypsy's nose smelled out trouble

A large German shepherd was hiding among the flat cars, where I worked at the Canadian Pacific Railway piggyback terminal in Winnipeg, Manitoba.

It was a cold winter's day in January, and not even the Humane Society people could catch her. I started sharing my lunch with her,

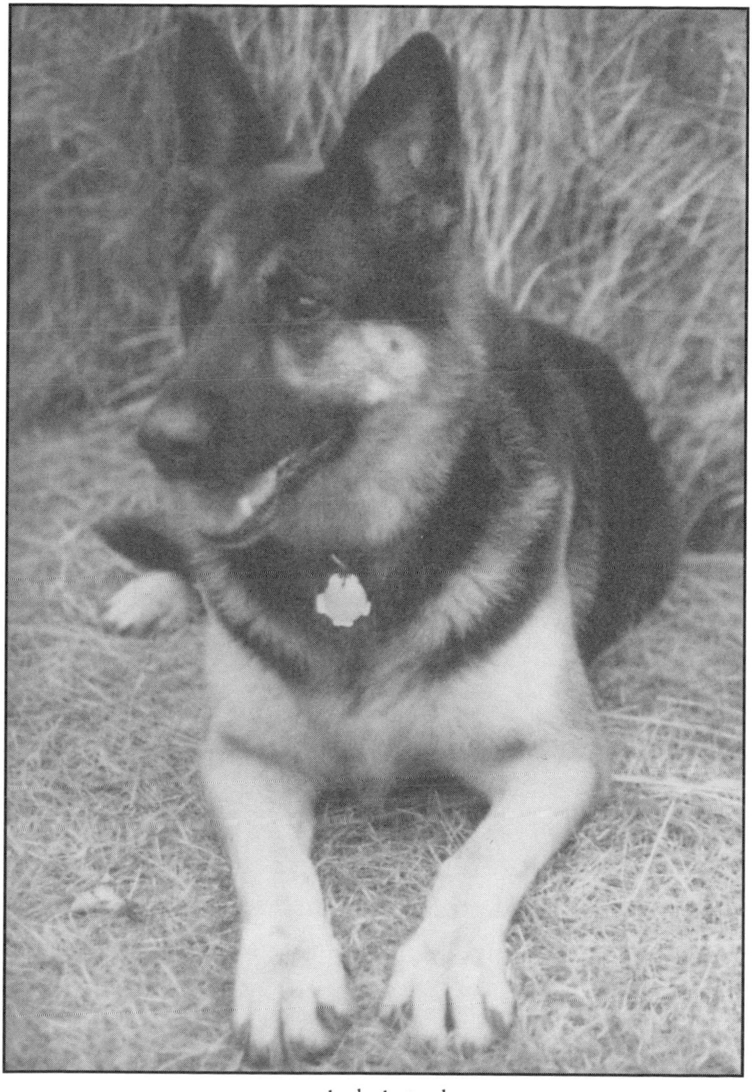

Gypsy Rose looked after her master

and gradually she came to trust me enough to go home with me on Valentine's Day. I named her Gypsy Rose.

She learned many tricks, and by fall became my goose-hunting retriever. After my shift I gathered my hunting equipment and my dog, and off we went in my truck with a slide-in camper. After a two-and-a-half-hour drive we reached my favorite secluded hunting area near Dolly Bay, along Lake Manitoba.

I turned on the propane gas but decided I was too tired to make coffee, so went up to my bed over the cab and fell asleep.

Gypsy somehow managed to climb up to the bed. She whined, clawed and licked my face until I could hardly breathe. I got down and went out into the fresh air, feeling sick. When I felt a little better, we returned to Winnipeg and I went to see my doctor. He told me I could have died if I'd stayed in the propane fumes any longer. It took me a week to return to normal health.

Gypsy saved my life, for which my family is forever grateful.

Percy Roberts
Balmoral, Manitoba
Canada

Sally

Sally was a Scotch Border collie, tan, white and gold, with a lovely long thick coat. She was not young, she limped with arthritis and her master had retired her from working the sheep. Her gentle nature made her a marvelous pet.

About 30 years ago I was spending a summer holiday in Gisborne with friends. They had seven children and I had brought my three mischief makers. Mix together a warm summer, a six acre property to roam around, a couple of dogs, a horse and plenty of fruit trees to raid, and ten youngsters had a whale of a time.

One day, just before we all went for a picnic, Sally arrived with her family. As we had plenty of food, we invited them to come along. Three carloads went to the beach. The kids tumbled out of the car like puppies and raced to the sea, Sally in the middle, joyfully barking. After a swim and a paddle, building sandcastles and digging ditches (Sally was the best digger), it was time for lunch. A spot in front of a camping area was chosen because the grass gave us a clean eating space.

My youngest daughter Megan had just learned to walk. No sitting down for her. Biscuit in hand, she wandered off. Suddenly I noticed a little black dog approaching the baby, beady eyes on the biscuit. Before I could get up, Sally was there, gently pushing her body between Megan and the black dog and enticing the stranger away for a play.

I remarked on this incident to Sally's master.

'She's retired now but she was the best sheepdog I ever had. She's also very good with children.' He sounded proud of her achievements.

The lunch finished in peace ... hot sun, good food, good company and the smell and sound of the sea. I started to relax – but not for long. Megan had taken off again. It was amazing how fast such a small scrap could move.

The camping area consisted simply of a dirt track, a long row of small baches and a gate. The gate couldn't close and there were no fences around it. It was just there, a gate into nowhere.

Megan was nearly through the gate. I made a move to get up but Sally's master stopped me.

'Let Sally get her. After all, a stray lamb or a stray baby is about the same. Just watch.' He raised his voice. '*Sally – baby – fetch.*' And his arm pointed toward the child.

Sally was off. She caught up with Megan and planted her big body in front of the child. Megan stopped, patted Sally, then moved to pass in front of the dog. Sally moved forward, blocking the exit and at the same time she shoved. Very gently, but she shoved. Megan decided to pass the dog at the tail end. Sally backtracked, blocked that exit and shoved again, persistently. Megan turned back, retracing her steps. As she reached the first bach she was distracted and veered off track to her new discovery. Sally's body blocked her again and Sally shoved. It was amazing to watch. Shove to the left, shove to the right, push ahead and shove again.

The little one gave up and toddled back to us, Sally walking behind her with a proud and proprietary air.

Ines Helberg
Auckland
New Zealand

Bogie was a good judge of character

My friend's daughter returned home from her summer job at the local shopping center with a roly-poly puppy who had a strange ridge on his back. She advertised locally but no one claimed him. We named him Bogie after Humphrey Bogart.

He grew into a formidable-looking dog with a huge chest and powerful neck. Despite his appearance, he was gentle and loved tummy rubs. We felt completely safe with Bogie on guard. At our remote ranch in northern California, he warned us of a murderous scoundrel in our midst.

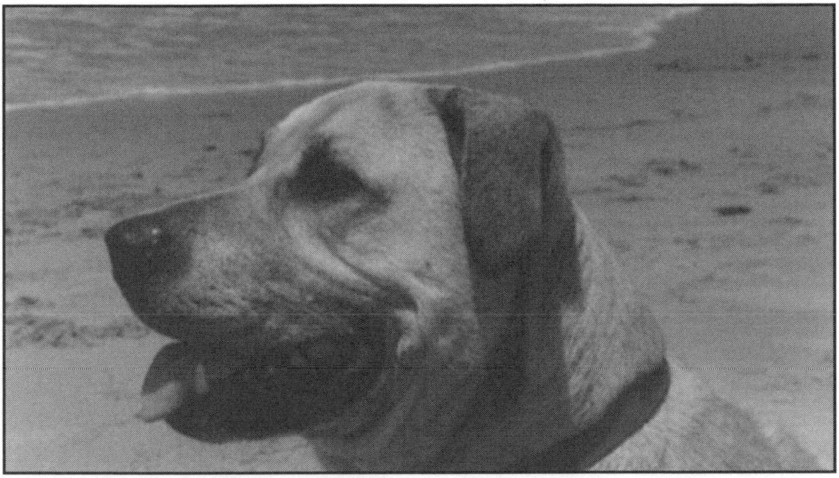

Bogie could sense the miner's true nature

One of the miners on the river had a shady reputation but we thought him harmless. He often took a short cut through our land on his way to and from his claim. He would stop for water or a soda, and talk with my husband and the caretaker.

On one occasion, Bogie wouldn't stop growling at this man. I stayed in the cabin with my daughter, and my husband Will had to finish his conversation outside because of the dog's behavior. I heard the man protest, 'I don't understand. Dogs usually like me.' He finally left, and Bogie continued to growl at the door.

Later that week, the sheriff's deputies hiked two and a half miles off the end of the road looking for the miner. We knew he'd had scrapes with the law and was wanted on marijuana and traffic warrants in Florida. I said jokingly to the officers, 'Boy, you fellas sure came a long way to serve a few warrants.'

They replied, 'It's a little more serious than that, ma'am. We think he shot his mining partner and tried to dynamite rock to cover the body.'

From that day forward, I never questioned Bogie's judgment of character.

Sharon Johnson
Belmont, California
United States

Write to me ...
email Sharon
billsharj@comcast.net

She scratched frantically at the shower door

My dog Jeze accompanies me everywhere. One night after we returned from ministry I wanted a shower, and turned on the television – just for a bit of noise for her, not even noticing what was on. Suddenly I became aware that she was growling, and scratching frantically at the shower door. She'd disappear to the living room and then return, repeating her scratching and growling more urgently.

When I stepped from the shower, Jeze grabbed the hem of my robe and pulled me toward the back door, making frantic growling sounds. It wasn't until I saw the television that I realized she must have been reacting to a house fire that was a scene in the movie.

I believe Jeze was adamant that she was going to rescue me and nothing would stop her. It wasn't until I'd grabbed the remote and turned off the TV that she ceased her efforts to save me. So much for dogs not being able to watch television.

Margaret Richardson
Blackburn South, Victoria
Australia

A spur of the moment adoption

Jessie was a spur of the moment adoption, being taken to the pound after spending a month in a crate because her first adoptive family had tired of the responsibility of a puppy.

She was a shepherd/collie cross, probably with a few other breeds in there as well. We soon understood why the family was willing to part with her – she was a handful. Despite what I had been told, she was not house-trained, nor did she understand one word of the human language, including 'No'. We were glad that we had bought

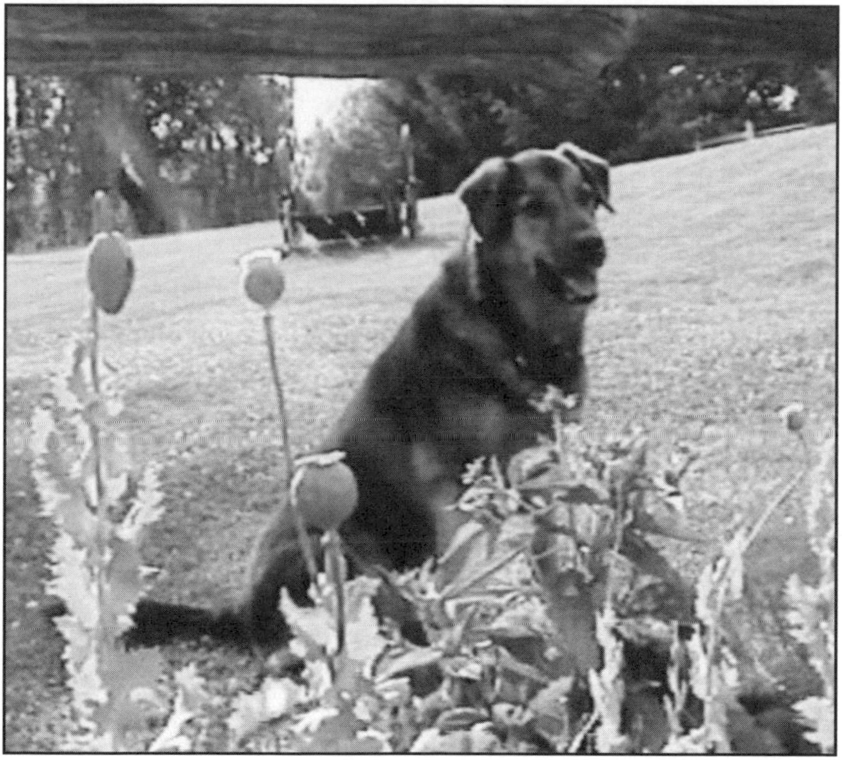

Jessie alerted her family to danger

her crate as well, for she would go to it when she was tired and grant us a reprieve from her enthusiasm. Eventually she became well behaved, with a minimal amount of 'selective hearing'.

We moved to an old house in the country when she was two, and we were sure she thought she was in paradise.

We always sleep with the bedroom door closed as we have three cats and my husband is allergic to them. One night, Jessie was moaning gently outside our bedroom door. She would make a little 'yip' sound and then moan again.

We told her to shush. She did for a few minutes, but then started again. We got up to see what she wanted, since her behavior wasn't typical. She went with us downstairs and into the kitchen by the stove. There was a switch at the front of the oven for a fan and it was making an odd buzzing noise, with an alarming smell emanating from it like electrical wiring that was burning.

My husband shut off the power to the kitchen, and with the help of a few tools he took the switch completely out of the stove. Jessie sat and watched, and when it was completed she headed back upstairs to bed. We are sure she prevented what could have become a real danger.

Sandy Neilly
Hastings, Ontario
Canada

3

Smart animals learn fast

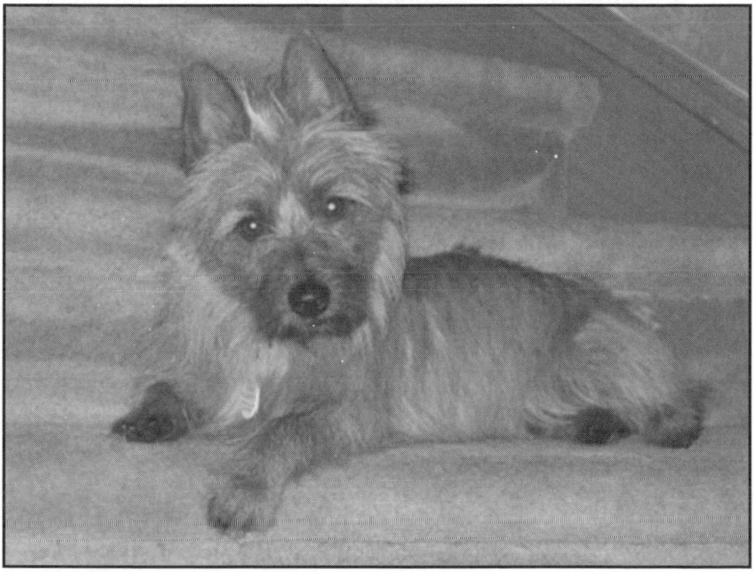

Chauncey quickly associated plastic bags with a walk

She's got a plastic bag, it must be time for a walk

Australian terriers have owned my husband and me for over 30 years. They have a wonderful personality and are a joy to live with.

A few years ago we would occasionally babysit a third Aussie, Chauncey, for a friend. From the beginning, Chauncey showed the quick intelligence that is characteristic of the breed.

Every morning I go for a long walk by myself. Afterwards I usually put my socks in my sneakers by the door, or upstairs on the bed to wear later in the day when I take the dogs for their walk. The sneakers are close to where I keep the leashes, and the plastic bags used for pick-up duties on the dog walks.

On one of his early stays with us, I noticed that whenever I had a plastic bag in my hand, even when simply unpacking groceries, Chauncey would run to fetch my socks from the sneakers. If by chance the socks weren't there, he'd race up to the bedroom and snatch them from the bed. Then he'd run to me, drop the socks at my feet, and look expectantly at the bag and over to the leashes, leaping and bouncing with excitement, ready for his walk.

The first time I was a little puzzled by his actions, as he was only a seven-month-old pup and I thought it was an accident. But he continued to fetch my socks on this and all subsequent visits with us.

Chauncey has moved away and now I have to fetch my own socks, but I still think of him whenever I find myself with a plastic bag in my hand.

Maree Graham
Kitchener, Ontario
Canada

The three Siamese who'd had enough

Thirty years ago when I was a young teenager, I was blessed with the companionship of three Siamese cats whom I had named Ting, Ming and Ling. They were different color types – tabby point, chocolate point and lilac point. Two were distantly related. All had very different personalities. Their capers and escapades were a constant source of amusement and joy, and I miss them still.

At one time in our street a new family moved in, and the two little girls often accompanied their mum down to the corner shop. Then, a little while after this, this family acquired a young and silly Alsatian and he was sent down the road with the little girls – unleashed.

Our front gates did not often get closed, so the first I knew of the Alsatian's arrival was when three flashes of white lightning streaked up the driveway and bolted up various trees at the back. It was Ting, Ming and Ling getting away from the marauding dog. The Alsatian had great fun every time it came down the street, crossing hither and thither, chasing everything it could – especially my poor cats. They did look funny – fur all puffed up, with their tails turned into bottlebrushes – but it was stressful for them, particularly for the little lilac point female.

Then one day I was standing on our enclosed front veranda when the little girls wandered down the opposite side of the street with their nuisance dog. The three cats just happened to be in the small front yard on the driveway, all close together.

As usual the dog rushed over, but stopped dead at the driveway entrance – its front legs splayed out, head down and tongue lolling, ready to pounce. At this moment the cats, in perfect synchronization, turned to face the dog. I couldn't believe my eyes because then, like cowboys before a gunfight, they slowly and deliberately marched down the drive, tails erect, hackles up and fur puffed out as far as possible. There they were, shoulder to shoulder in a line, in order of size from largest to smallest – Ming, Ting, then Ling. Goodness knows what their faces looked like, as I was witnessing this from above.

The dog, staying in pounce position, watched for some moments, then turned and fled! Other things occasionally frightened my cats, but never again did that Alsatian cross the street to visit us.

Susheela Millburn
Buderim, Queensland
Australia

I'd better catch the bus home

Sally, our black and tan terrier, loved to be taken out in the family car. Even when it was stationary, she would sit for hours on the back seat, apparently determined that if anyone was going anywhere they wouldn't go without her.

She was in luck that morning as I had to shop for groceries. 'Hi, Sal,' I acknowledged as I leaped in the car and headed for the nearest town, about ten miles away. When we got to the car park I made sure the window was open to give her plenty of fresh air. I then hurried off to do my shopping.

I came back, loaded the groceries into the boot and started off. It wasn't until I was nearly home that I realised Sally wasn't in the car. Oh no! Panic stations. She must have wanted to spend a penny, and got out through the window.

By this time, huge black thunderclouds had formed and the first few large drops of rain started to fall. I turned the car around and headed back to town through an ever-increasing storm. Where to look for her?

I checked the car park but she was nowhere to be seen, so I drove slowly through the deluge and down the main street. To my delight, I spotted her – sitting patiently at the end of a long bus queue.

I tooted the horn, and a line of wet and bedraggled people looked expectantly in my direction. As I stopped the car, their expressions were hopeful, only to be replaced by sheer disbelief as a rather wet but happy dog was ushered into the back seat and driven home in style.

Thea Pond-Jones
Dorset
England

Write to me ...
email Thea
thea.pondjones@tiscali.co.uk

Rocks in his head

It was a hot day in the wheat belt town of Moora, Western Australia, and I had collected a ute-full of rocks to build rock rings round the trees in our front yard. Each was about the size of a human head. I dropped the tailgate, grabbed a couple of rocks, threw them over near the first tree, grabbed a couple more and walked over to start laying them around the tree.

Leaving a half meter radius, I began the circle by laying the first four rocks. I turned to go and get more rocks, and tripped over one. I picked it up, placed it in the circle, turned and tripped over another.

Were the rocks multiplying at my feet?

I looked up to see Butch, my favorite hound, jumping into the ute. Now, that jump in itself was a feat. Butch may have the face of an Old English sheepdog, but he has the body length and short legs of a dachshund – albeit, just as gray and hairy as an Old English.

I watched from behind the tree.

He nosed a rock off the back of the ute, jumped down, and proceeded to find the best way to grip it with his teeth. Then he lifted and carried it, with his head at the most awkward angle, only to drop the rock in front of the tree I was working at.

I continued to watch from behind the tree. Back he went to go through the same procedure.

Between us we built three rockeries that afternoon. When we had finished, I grabbed a cold beer and turned on the sprinklers for Butch. He had earned a shower.

He was, and still is, the best apprentice I ever had.

Dave Bowen
Mandurah
Western Australia

Write to me ...
email Dave
dbbooks@westnet.com.au

Guess why we called her Flash

'Dad, Dad, come quick, there's a cat in the chook house.' My son Liam burst into the house, yelling out the news. 'You've got to come quick and catch it.'

I followed him to the chicken coop. A small feral tabby kitten was hunched in one corner, while a bunch of chooks clucked and flapped in the other. The kitten was hissing, growling and spitting all at once, which I thought was an impressive effort.

After a fair bit of chasing around, I had it. I carried the snarling wheeze bag out of the chicken coop and headed up to the house. Quite what I thought I was going to do with this animal eluded me. I just knew I had to show my wife Sharon (a fanatical cat lover) what had caused the excitement. Thirty yards into the trip, it managed to spin around in my hand, bite me through my fingernail and mark me in the arm with its claws.

Bravely carrying on, I arrived at the back door and yelled for assistance. None was forthcoming, except for some oohing and aahing about how sweet it looked dangling from what remained of my left arm.

Eventually I extracted the kitten from my shredded arm, promised faithfully that I wouldn't aid its shuffling off this mortal coil (I had what was left of my fingers crossed so am not sure if this promise counted) and locked it in the annex with food and water. Sharon continued to try to tame it, and slowly it calmed down. You could very nearly get close if you moved as slowly as a sloth having a lie-in. But the worst was yet to come.

Sharon was preparing my favorite dinner, pork chops. I was fetching the wine in anticipation when it happened. Sharon placed my pork chop into an extremely hot frying pan. The sizzling sound was sensational and the fat put up a great show of leaping into the air.

Thump! In through the kitchen window came the cat. Across the bench, over the sink and into the pan, grabbing the pork chop on the way. Out the other side, back through the hot frying pan and out of the kitchen the same way it came in, my pork chop clamped firmly between its teeth. We just stood there, hungry but amazed. I'd never seen anything move so fast. So what happened next? Well, I had a sandwich for tea and Sharon had fish.

The cat was eventually tamed and became a loved member of the family. Her name came to us pretty easily: she was a Flash in the pan.

Stan Barnett
Onewhero, South Auckland
New Zealand

Write to me ...
Stan Barnett
36 Kauri Road
RD2, Onewhero
South Auckland 1892
NEW ZEALAND

Bonnie gets ready for bed

One step ahead of the game

Bonnie, my Jack Russell terrier, loves to go through the fence next door as she knows she will get a treat there.

I stopped that game but she found another one. She still goes next door, but then barks like mad and runs back into my house. She keeps on barking until my neighbor calls out to see if anything's wrong.

'Is her barking driving you mad?' I say, and my neighbor replies, 'No, Bonnie wanted me to follow her to your house.' She had rushed over, thinking I must have fallen again. 'Right,' I said, 'she now has both of us on a piece of string, knowing she'll get a treat that way.'

But now I've become as cunning as her, by saying, 'I'm going to work', so that she gives a sigh and lies down in her basket. So we're one up on her – that is, until she gets another idea. Oh, don't think

I don't love her! She is all I have now, and at the age of 80 I would be lost without her. All I need to say is 'I'm going to bed', and what happens? She is there before me with her teddy.

Mrs Thelma Guppy
Middlesex
England

Watch and learn

I never really thought too much about possums and whether they were intelligent or not. But one night one particular brushtail possum certainly made me sit up and take notice of the species.

I was camping out in Croajingalong National Park at Tamboon Inlet and we had transported our food via kayaks in a large watertight barrel with a screw-top lid. In the middle of dinner this very bold possum lingered around us, obviously after some food. It approached the barrel, realizing this was where the treasure lay, and tried to bite and scratch the barrel to get to the food. We then interrupted the possum to fetch some food out of the barrel, screwed the lid back on and sat back down.

To our amazement the possum reapproached the barrel and, instead of scratching and biting the barrel, it now tried to grab the lid with both paws and open it just as it had seen the humans do! It didn't have any luck as those little paws just couldn't quite do the job that was necessary, but it certainly gave it a good try.

Jenny Hourigan
Mordialloc, Victoria
Australia

Trust

Sitting at the table one night I noticed a little tiny spider, about as big as the small fingernail on an adult hand, standing near my book.

He (or she) didn't look right, and when I got my magnifying glass out I could see that his front legs were totally bound together by a spider's web. It was wound around tightly. It looked like he'd got his feet caught in a web and he'd spun around and around before escaping. Poor little bugger.

I got a needle and my magnifying glass and very slowly and carefully began pulling the web away from his front legs. His legs were much skinnier than cotton so, as you can imagine, I was very careful.

It took about half an hour to free him. At first he tried to escape, holding his little bound legs in the air, because he thought I was trying to hurt him. But after ten minutes or so he was hooking the web and levering himself back away from the needle and working the web off himself. The dear little creature was using the needle as a tool to free himself. Now, that is a smart little thing!

Hannah Grace
Mullumbimby, New South Wales
Australia

Write to me ...
Hannah Grace
21 Gordon Street
Mullumbimby NSW 2482
AUSTRALIA

4

Smart animals to the rescue

Different ways of speaking

It was winter, it was cold and I was late: driving north along the Auckland motorway in the rush hour, trying to decide what to cook for dinner.

But I saw him. A little foxie, on the grass verge to my left, about two meters back from the tarmac. He sat facing the traffic noise and fumes. Waiting. And I knew it.

He was waiting so hard and with a faith so absolute that we connected. He knew we would. Me, or someone. He didn't mind how long it took. I found myself taking the next off-ramp, circling the roundabout to drive south, onto the next on-ramp at Otahuhu and up the motorway again.

He was still there. We both knew he would be. He ran to meet me, tail wagging, tongue panting in relief. *I knew you'd come!* I switched off the ignition and got out, following as he ran down toward a soggy shallow stream. *This way, come on!* Looking back to make sure I did.

I squelched after him, to see a second small dog half standing in the water, apparently to reassure a third dog, lying in the muddy stream. She was trapped, on her side, a front paw wedged in a rusty

metal spring. I knelt down by her, a dog each side to urge me on as I gently lifted her onto the grass, the better to try and free her.

It wasn't easy. The coil was heavy and the four of us seemed to hold our collective breath until finally I managed it. I massaged her paw to restore the circulation, and she licked my hand. I stood the patient up. She shook herself wetly, and then all three – with a final canine thank you – happily took off, up the grassy bank beyond the stream. Mission accomplished. And I was going to be late with dinner.

Dogs talk, all right. All animals do. It's just that they have different ways of speaking, and too often we don't listen.

Olwen Macrae
Woodend, North Canterbury
New Zealand

A stallion and a barn cat

Our Arabian stallion developed a close relationship with a barn cat during a cold winter in Saskatchewan, Canada.

We would go into the barn in the morning to see the cat curled up on the horse's back, warm and comfortable. The horse would just stand there, apparently trying not to disturb the sleeping cat.

One morning, though, the stallion was lying down and didn't get up when the barn door opened. This alarmed us, since horses usually stand, especially at feeding time. We looked in to see the horse with its head on its outstretched front feet, staring into the corner.

The cat had just given birth to several kittens and the horse was intently watching over the birthing scene. The mother cat kept her delicate offspring safely in the stallion's box stall for several weeks, and he took care not to step on any of the babies.

The cat moved her kittens only when they started to roam too freely around the stallion's legs.

Mark Husband
Dauphin, Manitoba
Canada

The gulls were the winners

Lake Horowhenua is a great place for birdlife. They know they are protected and that friendly motorists with cars full of ankle-biters will occasionally pull up and feed them from bags of bread.

I was sitting in the car, knitting as always, when I glanced toward the lake. He with the camera was out there, taking photos of pukekos doing their loopy walk on the grass.

As I watched, I saw a hawk circling several ducks. It swooped on a half-grown duckling, and with one mighty leap the mother duck shot up in the air toward the hawk.

The hawk flew up but came back for another attack. The same thing happened; the mother duck again took the hawk on. After another attempt, the hawk gave up and flew up and over the reeds to head toward the far side of the lake.

Immediately, two seagulls took off after the hawk and proceeded to beat the bird lower down toward the water. The hawk broke free and flew upwards, but again the gulls pushed the bird toward the lake. Eventually, the hawk escaped the gulls' attentions and flew away.

I watched as two satisfied gulls came back to where the ducks were, circled them, making a mighty cawing sound and then did a few acrobatic loops. I had the feeling they were saying to themselves, *Gulls – 1, hawk – 0.*

I was fascinated with the battle between waterfowl and land/air-based birds.

Babs Spencer
Lower Hutt
New Zealand

Coppa was trying to tell me something

It was early one morning and I was getting ready for work when I heard my Labrador puppy Coppa barking at the back door.

She was just finding her voice, and hadn't barked before. I told her she was a clever girl, but that wasn't the end of it. She kept on barking and getting very worked up.

I started to wonder why two-year-old Jess wasn't barking too. I went outside to look, and eventually spotted her down the back garden. I called out but she didn't move, and when I went up to her I saw she was tangled up in some garden fence wire. We had to cut her free with pliers as the wire was wrapped around her chest and front legs.

I realised that little Coppa had been trying to tell me that Jess needed our help.

Mrs G Weir
Morely
Western Australia

Jess and her hero Coppa

A clever sheep to the rescue

I once knew a clever sheep called Annie. She'd been bottle-fed, then put out into a paddock that came up to the house fence so we could still keep in touch with her.

It was an interesting paddock, with a gully, hills, creek and willows, and Annie had the company of her friend Mabel who'd been given to us by a family that moved house and couldn't take her with them.

One morning I heard Annie calling out at the front fence. She did sometimes call if she saw one of us but this was different, it sounded urgent. I went to investigate. She was standing at the fence, staring toward the house and baaing. Mabel wasn't in sight, which was unusual as they were normally not far apart.

I climbed through the fence, and together we went out to the top of the slope going down to the creek. And there, down in the creek, bogged in the watercress, was Mabel. Annie knew she needed help for Mabel and she knew where to go for it.

Jean Campbell
Havelock North
New Zealand

Honey asks her humans for help

Honey, our miniature mare, gave birth to a darling little foal. He weighed ten kilograms at birth and was fit and well.

Unfortunately, the same could not be said for Honey. The following day she developed a high temperature and, to keep an eye on her, we brought her closer to the house. She was used to grazing around the swimming pool so that was where we put her.

At three days old, Little Tex stood a mere 13 inches high and presented an enchanting picture just asking to be filmed. I decided to video the pair.

I'd been filming for a few minutes, when I was horrified to see – through the viewfinder – Tex put a tiny hoof on the edge of the pool and slip in. As with most accidents it happened so quickly. One minute he was a safe distance from the pool and the next he was in the water.

I dropped the camera and ran around the left side of the pool. Honey couldn't have seen me, as she ran around the right side and up onto the patio. She thrust her front hooves into the doorway and neighed for help.

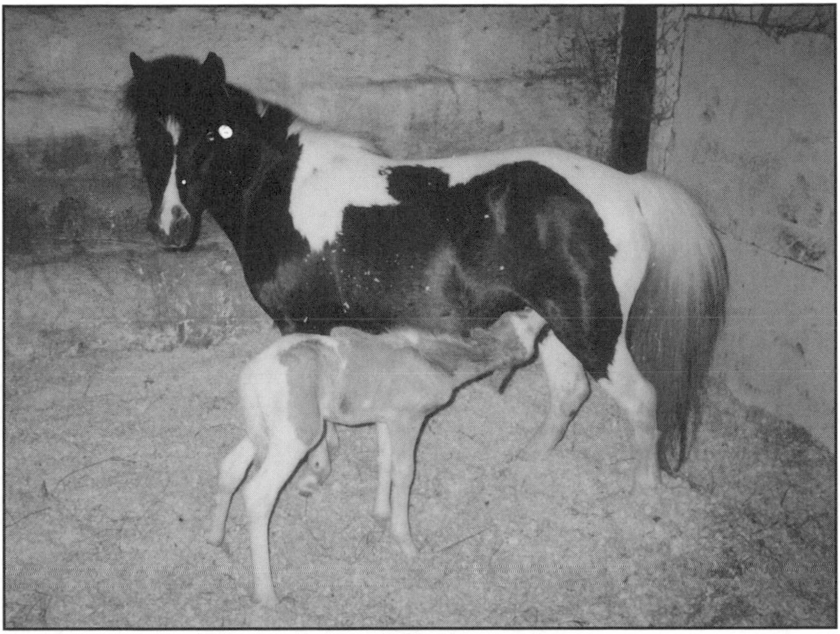

Honey sought help for her son Little Tex

I shouted, 'I'm here, Honey' and she came trotting to me. She stood close while I pulled Tex out and dried him. I'm sure she was grateful that I had been on hand to save her baby.

We've had horses whinny to let us know when one of them has escaped from the paddock, but never anything as obvious as Honey running to the door to call for help.

Three days later, I'm sad to say Honey died. She lost her battle with the infection that had developed the day after Little Tex was born. There's nothing quite so pathetic as an orphan foal no higher than your knee, but we pulled him through. He is now a strapping two-year-old who spends his days romping with his dad. I am regarded as the mother in our little herd, even by Dad, who protects me by nipping Little Tex when he gets a bit above himself.

Every time I look at him I'm reminded of his intelligent mum who thought to ask her human family for help.

Darlene Bond
Ashburton, KwaZulu, Natal
South Africa

Fisher quacked instructions

It was spring and my brother wanted a new project. He was tired of the usual farm chores … looking after the horses, cows and pigs, and taking his turn to cut down trees, limbing, sawing and splitting wood.

He rode his bike about three miles to a neighbor's place, where he bought six duck eggs. He gave them to a hen and she sat for weeks, turning the eggs several times a day, leaving them only long enough to have some food, and clucking at them as mothers do in any family. This was her way of letting them know she'd be a good mother when they arrived. Finally, one egg hatched.

The duckling was on his own – almost. My brother and I fished polliwogs out of a nearby pond several times a day. He could eat them faster than we could get them, but we fished until the frogs came in place of the little creatures. Then we gave him hen scratch and a name, Fisher.

Later that summer, Wayne went to the city of Halifax to work. Fisher went to the pasture with the cows. Every day, my father put the cows in the barn to milk and feed them. He put scratch in the Jersey cow's stall for Fisher before coming in for supper, after which he and I went to the wood lot, where he split wood and I stacked it.

One afternoon Fisher came to the wood lot, making a real fuss. My father basically told him to get lost. Then the duck came to me. 'Dad, he wants you to follow him,' I said.

'Oh my God, the cow must have had her calf. Tell your mother to get the wheelbarrow and come. I'll go with him.' Mother did as instructed, while I stayed at the wood lot.

When suppertime came, Father went to get the other cow. He could hear her call before she surfaced over the top of the hill. He could also hear Fisher's quacking guidance as he brought the cow down over the hill. The hill was steep, so Father took them back and forth across it so they wouldn't stumble. Fisher did this daily until the animals were sold a few years later.

The folks held some card games, and in the first game Fisher became first prize. The fellow who won him intended to have roast duck. Some 20 years later, I found out that he hadn't been able to kill him after all. They went to the woods for a walk each day, and eventually Fisher became the leader, waddling ahead of his new owner and giving his quacking instructions. I was glad to hear that he eventually died of old age.

Joyce L Cook
Upper Tantallon, Nova Scotia
Canada

Write to me ...
Joyce Cook
13175 Peggys Cove Road
Upper Tantallon NS B37 2J8
CANADA

Brandy and Jasper enjoy a nap together

They look out for each other

After a deck renovation, we added a set of garden doors with lever-type handles. For several nights we noticed that it was getting chilly in the house, and found a garden door open each time.

My husband and I blamed each other for not shutting the new door tightly. Finally we caught the real culprit. It was our house cat Chester.

He'd learned that, if he climbed up the center post between the garden doors and hung onto the handle, it opened the door when he wanted to come in. We noticed that the other house cats and our dog waited for him to do this so that they too could come in when they wanted.

We changed the handles to the knob type. But since then, our other house cat, Jasper, has started yowling at us. When we go to see what he wants, our dog Brandy is waiting at the garden door to come in. Brandy immediately climbs on the couch and Jasper lies down beside her.

In turn, Brandy has woken us up with whining and scratching at our bed, and when we go to the garden door Jasper is waiting to come in. Our guess is that our pets look out for one another.

Mary J Marzyk
Dauphin, Manitoba
Canada

A soul in need

One hot Tuesday afternoon in February 2000, I was walking home from my friend Natasha's place. Just as I reached my front gate, my four-year-old Doberman cross bitch Timothy Anjelika jumped the eight plus foot high fence surrounding the backyard.

At first, I thought she was just super-happy to see me. But instead of jumping up on me, Tim raced past me and across the four lanes that make up Francis Street, a very busy truck route – especially at 4 pm, peak hour.

'Oh, s*#@!' I yelled in shock, as my dog had her lovely black tail whacked by a passing sedan. Still standing at the gate, I dropped my bag and ran after Tim, narrowly missing being knocked down myself. I followed Tim as she ran about 500 meters up the footpath and turned in at the gate to the Westgate golf course. I kept following. We both ran across the neatly mowed green grass and, although angry golfers were screaming at her, Tim kept running.

I was running as fast as I could, but there was no way I was going to catch up to her. After running for about a kilometer, I saw that we were approaching a section of Stony Creek which passes through the golf course. Tim saw it too, but did that stop her? No way! While still running, Tim half-crouched and leaped, easily clearing the seven foot wide creek. A slight stumble might deter some dogs, but not my Timothy – she kept going. I followed on, after crossing the little wooden bridge that enables golfers to access both sides of the course.

We ran and ran, ignoring the verbal abuse from many golfers. After running a speed and distance that would leave any racing greyhound for dead, Timmy leaped into Stony Creek where it first enters the golf course, right under the Williamstown Road on-ramp for the Westgate bridge.

'Okay, now what's she up to?' I wondered, as I struggled to make the distance that my dog so easily had.

Finally I reached the edge of the creek and, with all the breath I could muster, I called to Timmy. Then I noticed that she was dragging something white in her mouth as she half-swam, half-waded through the murky brown, polluted water. When she reached the bank she scrambled up, dropped the plastic bag at my feet and shook herself.

'What's that, Tim?' I asked, as I crouched down and peered inside the now torn bag. What I saw made me so angry. Inside the shopping bag was a lifeless grey and white kitten. Although I was sure it was dead, I picked it up and began rubbing it with my windcheater.

Meow, the little creature cried, as it looked up at me with its big yellow-green eyes before closing them again.

'Come on, Tim,' I said to my dog, my hero. She was sitting at my feet, looking up at me and whining. This was very unusual for her; she hates me paying attention to any other animals.

As we made our way home, I was worried about Tim not having her leash on. But I needn't have: she heeled better than any dog ever could. Not even a dog with a utility dog title could have performed better. Ignoring the rude golfers, we finally made it home.

The first thing I did was put the kitten in my own cat's carry box, with some food, water and cat milk. The grey and white thing turned out to be a 14-week-old British shorthair, a very frightened, wet and muddy one at that.

After organizing my then one-year-old Angelus (a black male Burmese/American shorthair cross), Timothy, and the other three dogs – one of which was my then three-month-old Newfoundland pup Spike – I rang Mum at work and explained the situation. She came home immediately and drove the kitten and me to the Lord Smith Animal Hospital, where the kitten stayed overnight.

The next day, Mum and I went back to the animal hospital and adopted the poor little kitten. We named her Buffy, after Buffy the Vampire Slayer, so that she would go nicely with Angelus. On the TV show, Buffy and Angel dated for a while.

Three years have passed since that eventful day. Buffy's best friends are Angelus and Spike, since Buffy is only two weeks older than Spike. For all her trouble, Timothy Anjelika (now almost eight years old) was given the RSPCA's award for outstanding achievement. It was presented to her at the 2000 RSPCA Million Paws Walk by RSPCA president Dr Hugh Wirth.

One thing I am still unclear about is how did Tim know about Buffy? The little thing was dumped a kilometer and a half away from my backyard, where Tim was. Maybe I should call in the X-Files?

Elsa Hoggard
Yarraville, Victoria
Australia

A pig's devotion to her sister

I have two pet kunekune pigs known as Bacon and Eggs. They are sisters and the best of friends.

A couple of years ago, Bacon went missing in the bush. Despite constant calling and a thorough search we couldn't find her. Eggs still came to the gate religiously for a feed in the evening, which we found strange.

Fearing the worst, I asked some friends to help me conduct one last search. We found Bacon not far from home, pinned under the branch of a tree. Around her was a nest of freshly pulled grass that her sister Eggs had made for her.

After much pulling and tugging we managed to release Bacon from her tree. With careful nurturing, she survived to tell her remarkable tale of sisterly love.

Lesley Franklin
Onerahi, Whangarei
New Zealand

Devoted sisters Bacon and Eggs

Chilli's hero

Toby was an abandoned puppy I had welcomed into my home from the pound when he was six months old. We took a guess and figured his ancestry was possibly Labrador/Australian cattle dog.

He was a gentle soul who was truly grateful for being given a second chance at life with a new family, never letting us out of his sight. He loved playing with all other dogs and had his regular playmates at the park. One day, however, a neighbor's dog who disliked other dogs followed its owner onto our property. Toby, pleased to see a fellow four-legged friend, went to greet this dog with a wagging tail.

Suddenly, and to the shock of us all, with no warning signs this dog attacked Toby right in front of us. Terrified, Toby retreated to his bed and nursed his wounds.

From that moment on, Toby's carefree life was shattered. The twinkle left his eye when he saw other dogs he did not know, and he lived in fear of the neighbor's dog, which was close enough for him to be able to see, hear and smell on a daily basis.

Some years later Toby was given the opportunity to play older brother to an extremely active and wickedly intelligent German koolie puppy whom we called Chilli. At ten, Toby was getting on in age and he was quite reluctant to interact and try to tame the wild Chilli, avoiding all attempts by her to play and wrestle.

Chilli was determined to find somebody to play with and was most excited when she spied the neighbor's dog wandering on our property. With a cheerful yap, she took off after the neighbor's dog. Much to my horror, I could see the dog raise its hackles and start gnashing its teeth as it turned to charge. As quickly as I could, I started running toward our new pup in an attempt to save her from inevitable injury or even death. Heart thumping, my legs just were not getting me there quickly enough to save her. Then, to my

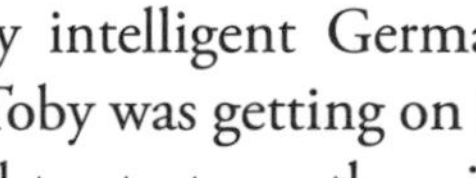

Toby and Chilli

complete astonishment, I heard a pounding on the ground behind me.

As I turned my head I caught sight of Toby running as fast as he could toward the neighbor's dog. Blood drained from my face as I expected a terrible dogfight to ensue, with the possibility of both of my beloved pets being injured.

Suddenly, there was this almighty thud with an expulsion of air. Toby had body-slammed the neighbor's dog, sending them up into the air and severely winding them both. While they lay on the ground regaining their breath, Chilli ran to me, tail between her legs, squealing in fear but with no physical injuries.

The neighbor's dog got up eventually, shook itself and cast a glance in Toby's direction. However, instead of standing at full dominating height it hung its head a bit and sauntered off with its tail hanging low.

Toby was winded but managed to drag himself back to the house, where Chilli promptly set about licking him all over. He didn't push her away – he was finally keen for her attention.

Chilli had a Hero!

Toby no longer retreated when he saw the neighbor's dog but would stand tall and be very alert. The neighbor's dog no longer comes onto our property. Toby lovingly took on the role of teacher and Chilli was a willing student. Toby is 14 now, is going blind and has terrible arthritis but he is still Chilli's Hero.

To this day, however, we are truly thankful for the courage Toby showed in the face of fear.

Julie Raverty
Echuca, Victoria
Australia

Ben was lost … until Amber turned up to save him

We got our dog Amber from the SPCA when she was four months old. She was a Labrador/collie cross and the color of her name, with a gentle nature.

At the age of 12, with arthritis in her back legs, she led a quiet life. She hated the rain and could 'hold on' for up to 48 hours before she'd go out in it. One night there was a stormy southerly and around 4 am Amber was awake and restless, pacing up and down the hall and by the front door. I couldn't believe she wanted to go out in that weather but she was agitated so I let her out.

Our back garden was very steep and the roadway was up the top. The garden was fenced all around; on one side was a strip of waste ground, full of trees, potholes, weeds and vines, and from the front door there were four deep concrete steps up to the main path. To the left was a narrow path leading toward a rockery and the waste ground. Between the fence and waste ground was a small gap, hardly a foot wide, before a five foot drop.

Next to the waste ground was a house occupied by a young man who had a blind Airedale called Ben. The young man was new to the area and was doing shift work. His routine had changed – as had Ben's, who didn't know if it was night or day and wanted to go out. His makeshift pen had been destroyed in the storm and Ben wandered off onto the waste ground. Tired from his shift, the young man had gone back to sleep.

Frightened, wet and cold, Ben was lost – until Amber ventured out. She walked along the narrow path until she came to the gap, where she barked a few times until Ben came toward her. Then she carefully turned around so that Ben could squeeze through the gap and follow her along the narrow path, down the steps to our front door. I dried them both, but to my amazement Amber wouldn't come inside but stayed with Ben in the porch until daylight.

I fed them dog biscuits for breakfast, when I heard a voice calling for Ben. I went up the path and found the young man. He came to collect Ben and was amazed to hear of Amber's heroic rescue.

Josephine Smith
Wellington
New Zealand

5

Smart animals get revenge and outwit us

Double-dipping

My late dog Suzzie, a Border collie/kelpie cross, would get a small food treat if she brought us some money.

From time to time she would find 20 cents here, 50 cents there.

One day at about 7 am, while I was still in bed, she brought 20 cents – so I gave her some of my toast. Then came 50 cents, so I gave her a bit more. Next came $1, followed by $2, then 50 cents.

By this time I was out of toast, and wondered where all the money was coming from.

I got up to find she had knocked over and broken the money box where I kept all the money she brought me.

Mandi Jayne
Mount Evelyn, Victoria
Australia

Caught in the act

Troya, our Labrador retriever, should have been named Houdini.

When she was six weeks old we would put her in our kitchen while we were at work. There was no door at either entrance, so

we placed a baby gate at one entrance and put her large crate at the other.

Every day when we came home she would be roaming freely through the house. My boyfriend and I could not for the life of us figure out how she got out, for nothing was out of place.

One day my boyfriend decided to trick her. He pretended to leave the house but instead he lay down very flat and still on the couch.

Sure enough, he heard a commotion in the kitchen and out came Troya, bouncing across the living room floor. He discovered that she'd been pushing her crate out of the doorway, just enough for her to wiggle through, and this is where the story gets interesting.

When Troya saw my boyfriend on the couch she scooted back to the kitchen, grabbed the crate by her teeth and pulled it back into place in the doorway. Nothing was out of place, the kitchen looked just as we'd left it and Troya looked like a little angel.

Tarragh Shanahan
Corner Brook, Newfoundland
Canada

Write to me ... ✉
email Tarragh
tarraghs@yahoo.ca

The gorilla's revenge

As I prepare to take my young son to the Melbourne Zoo, I recall a story my own mother told me of her visit to the zoo when she was a young Girl Guide.

Back in those days, many of the animal enclosures were small cages up on a platform, with bars across the front. They offered little environmental enrichment but allowed people to get near the animals.

My mother and her fellow Girl Guides took delight in getting up close to observe an enormous male gorilla who sat with his back to the crowd and appeared oblivious to the people watching him. Their fascination grew as they noticed that he was looking at his own reflection in a shiny hubcap-shaped dish that served as his food bowl.

A group of rowdy young Boy Scouts joined the crowd gathered around the gorilla's cage. They were either showing off in front of the Girl Guides or were bored by the gorilla's inaction, as they began to throw peanuts at the animal's back.

The Scouts' taunts proved fruitless as the gorilla continued his self-admiration in the shiny dish. After a short while, however, he placed his dish on the ground and ever so slowly began to scoop up the remains of his meal. It included mushy composting fruit and its peel. Along with these scraps, the gorilla scooped up his feces and collected them all in the dish.

All of a sudden, with lightning speed and incredible accuracy, the gorilla flung the contents of the dish over his shoulder to land right on his target, the rowdy Boy Scouts! They stood stunned, their uniforms covered in composted fruit and feces, while the crowd burst out laughing – none louder than my mother and her fellow Girl Guides.

It became clear that the gorilla had used the reflection in his dish to size up and accurately locate his tormentors. Everyone was impressed by this animal's use of tools and available resources to deliver his message in such a confined and limited environment. A great deal of laughter was shared, along with admiration for this creature with such dignity, poise and perfect comedic timing.

Julie Raverty
Echuca, Victoria
Australia

How to Boomer-proof a fridge

Early in Boomer's life he seemed to realize two very important 'facts': that he was really a human, not a cat; and that he loved eating more than anything else in the world.

Because of these two unalterable ideas, upon reaching adulthood Boomer appeared to make a conscious decision that he would not lower himself to the level of the other two felines in his household by consenting to eat only cat food (extremely boring!).

Unfortunately, his human 'pets' did not agree with his decision and continued to offer him only cat food (and 'lite' at that, because of their perceived idea that he had a weight problem). They continued to try his patience by keeping all the human food locked in a large white box they referred to as the 'fridge', and totally ignored all his reasonable requests for a higher standard of food.

Extreme measures were called for, so Boomer studied the problem carefully …

Several nights later, at an early hour in the morning, Dad was heard mumbling something about 'darned kid, leaving the fridge open again' … followed by a groan and then some colorful language, which included 'wretched cat!'. Dad had, after closing the fridge, walked in the darkness on something cold, wet and slimy on the living room carpet. It wasn't as bad as Dad had initially thought, though – it turned out to be a package of well-chewed Black Forest ham. Although Boomer had made the mistake of leaving the evidence behind (he didn't have time to eat it all before it was discovered), he had made sure that he himself was not in evidence, and seemed quite content to let Son take the blame for leaving the fridge open, making it easy for Boomer to get into it and help himself to a midnight snack.

After this type of thing happened a couple of times, however, Dad and Mom began to get suspicious – especially when the fridge happened to be open when neither Son nor Daughter was home. By this time, Boomer had expanded his horizons, sampling leftover steak, a two pound (900 gram) block of cheese, and some grapes (he didn't like those). He was much better at hiding the evidence, too – he now took his treats to the far corner of the basement, where his meal was less likely to be disturbed by inconsiderate humans.

It wasn't until Mom and Dad heard a four pound (1.8 kilogram) frozen roast hit the floor in the kitchen late one evening when neither kid was home that they finally clued in for sure – Boomer was the culprit! His serious daily study of the fridge, which they had assumed to be harmless, had paid off and he had figured out how to open it in order to help himself to the goodies it contained.

War was declared … a sort of one-sided war, as Boomer had still not been caught anywhere in the vicinity when the food 'happened' to fall out on the floor.

First of all, Dad thought that putting a chair in front of the fridge door would solve the problem. Boomer, however, being quite strong, merely skidded the chair out of the way (love those lino floors). Mom and Dad did catch a glimpse of this one day, when Boomer skidded the chair aside in the kitchen with his feline friend Pinky asleep on it at the time!

On to the next step. Dad thought that, if he smeared margarine laced with cayenne pepper around the door, when Boomer got it on his paws and licked it off the taste would cure him of going near the fridge forever. Wrong … Boomer loved the taste, and cleaned off the sides and bottom of the door as far up as he could reach!

Okay – third and more severe step … Mom and Dad made a 'tack belt' by forcing thumbtacks through tape and taping it along the side and bottom of the fridge, so that Boomer would poke himself when he tried to pull the door open. Boomer obliged by carefully ripping tiny sections of the tape off (complete with tacks

still attached) and scattering them around the kitchen floor, where Dad got to experience them when he walked barefoot through the kitchen on one of his midnight prowls (he really wasn't very happy with Boomer by this point in time).

Mom now realized just how serious the problem was, and went on a shopping expedition to see what remedy the retail sector could provide. She first tried attaching little sticky hooks on the side and front of the fridge and running elastic between them, rationalizing that, because they were out of Boomer's reach, he wouldn't be able to pull the door open. This worked well for a while, until the kids forgot to put the elastic back on after going into the fridge (and Boomer checked for this each time he walked through the kitchen). Then, after pulling on the door enough times each night, the little hooks could be persuaded to slide on the porcelain of the fridge and eventually would slide right off, allowing the door to be opened.

Mom headed back to the store and finally found a Boomer-proof lock, designed to keep children from being able to open oven doors. As the device locked automatically when the fridge door closed, Boomer could no longer depend on the kids forgetting to 'cat-proof' the fridge. Was he destined to enjoy only cat-type food again?

But wait ... what about all those other doors in the kitchen? Turns out there are all sorts of other human-type foods behind them, all neatly arranged on shelves, at just the right height for a slightly pudgy but very clever tabby cat (now nicknamed HippoBootamus by the kids) who really does like raisins, and nuts, and cereal, and ...

Laurie de Mille
Calgary, Alberta
Canada

A cockatiel's trickery

We're always trying to teach my whiteface cockatiel Piggy new things to say.

Every morning when my mum took off his covers she said, 'Good morning, Piggy.' And sure enough he soon said it back to her every morning.

But then he surprised us, and proved to me that he does know what the words mean and he's not just repeating them. After he had his cover on, he usually went silent, but now he says, *Good morning, Piggy* as soon as the cover goes on.

He lies to us, trying to make us think it is morning and time for his cover to come off again.

Bianca Dekker
Secret Harbour
Western Australia

Injun the enforcer

Injun was standing in the dappled shade of his favorite tree at the top of the hill in the paddock, which he shared with a number of other ponies and his best friend, Blackberry the donkey foal.

Injun loved anything smaller than himself, particularly children and donkeys. He was not a very brave pony but he was very benign, intelligent and gentle by nature.

He had spent a hard-working morning teaching children to ride. Three hours of solid concentration helping them try to do what the teacher demanded, followed by a cooling wash down from the hose and a good satisfying feed, accompanied by the lavish petting from the children.

He was happy and contented and wished only for a nice nap well out of the way of the other more rumbustious ponies, who would soon be let out into his paddock to spend the rest of the day playing rough games with each other and grazing.

Blackberry had spent the morning standing with his head over the fence, watching his big friend Injun working in the school arena. Near the end of the morning the girls came along with the hay and put a separate pile out for each of the ponies. Everyone loved the little chocolate brown donkey, and the staff were apt to spoil him with the biggest pile of the sweetest hay.

Blackberry immediately chose his pile and settled down to enjoy himself while all the ponies were still busy in the stable yard. On this day Injun was the first out, and Blackberry watched him trot off to his tree and realized that the others would soon be coming too and his peace would be shattered.

When the gate was opened the ponies erupted like rough boys let out of school, barging and jostling each other in their mad dash to get to their piles of hay. Blackberry tried to take no notice but to no avail, and he was soon forced to stand out of the way when one of the biggest ponies decided he wished to have that one particular pile. But what Blackberry lacked in weight and muscle, he more than made up for in brains. He could have gone to the spare pile, but he was very cross and annoyed and he did not see why he should be deprived of the pile he had chosen.

After a few moments of deep thought, Blackberry trotted off to ask Injun for help. They stood for a minute or two, nose to nose, while the matter was considered, and then Injun made his decision. Injun must have told Blackberry to stand well out of the way. Then he spent a little while practicing looking evil, pawing the ground like a bull and putting his ears flat back. And then he launched himself down the hill at full speed, with ears flattened and his evil facial expression.

The other ponies were clearly taken completely by surprise and did not wait to argue. They scattered in short time, leaving Injun to install his little friend Blackberry back on the pile of hay of his choosing. Having made sure that nobody was daring to argue, he turned on his heel and trotted back to resume his nap under the tree.

Anne Baulch
Wandin, Victoria
Australia

She who laughs last

My two Australian Silky terriers, Millie (five) and Jack (four), have been allowed to sleep on my bed over the years. Millie slept under the blankets, while Jack curled up near the pillows.

Things went smoothly for a long time but about six months ago, and without my noticing what was going on between them, Jack silently intimidated Millie into sleeping first at the end of the bed and then off it entirely. The result was that she was regularly sleeping in her own bed on the floor, where she seemed happy enough. Or so I thought!

It is often Jack's habit to scratch on the front door to be let out in the middle of the night, but one night in the cold early hours of the morning I heard Millie scratching loudly on the door. This was unusual behavior for her, as she generally likes to sleep through without disturbance. The scratching increased and I eventually motivated myself to get up into the cold night air. Jack followed me sleepy-eyed at my heels, for he rarely misses an opportunity to go outside.

With Millie scratching ever more determinedly, I hurried to reach her. As I raised my hand to turn the knob to let her out, she suddenly stopped scratching and raced to the empty bed where, with Jack (and me) safely out of the way, she happily hopped up under the blankets and settled down like she'd never missed a beat.

Georgina McLean
Tuggerawong, New South Wales
Australia

Millie and Jack

A resourceful rabbit

Smoky, our grey rabbit, lived at the bottom of the budgies' aviary.

The birds didn't seem to mind the intrusion – until Smoky decided that he rather liked budgie seed straight from the container rather than from the floor. My husband installed one of those seed bins that hook on the aviary wall, thinking that would solve the problem.

Smoky slept in a large upside down flowerpot. We heard a scraping sound coming from the cage, and saw Smoky pushing the flowerpot across to the new seed bin. Then he jumped on top of it so that he could reach the seed in the new holder.

Yes, he got to share it ever after. How could you deny such a clever animal a meal of birdseed?

Ivodell C Hyde
Murray Bridge
South Australia

Write to me ...
email Ivodell
ivodell@yahoo.com

Revenge of a peach-faced lovebird

My partner and I went into fits of giggles as we watched our peachface Floyd at her silly antics. Her clicks and chirps mimicked the tones of common words, so we knew when she was answering 'Goodnight' or saying 'Hello' because she changed the sound of her chirps to match the sound of each syllable. She could also mimic a great chuckle, which was always hilarious to hear.

We had a friend who used to tease Floyd. He would call her names and laugh at her, and if she perched on a rope he would wiggle it to unbalance her. We warned him not to tease her, as we were sure that one day Floyd would seek revenge.

One day she was playing in her favorite shoebox under the table. The box had a little doorway cut into it for her. Our friend walked into our flat and was about to talk to us. He suddenly let out a loud howl, swore and hopped about on one foot. We were just as surprised, as we couldn't see what he was making a fuss about. There was nothing there that he could have stood on.

When he calmed down, we heard Floyd's cheeky chuckle from inside the shoebox. It seems that, as soon as she heard his voice, she dashed out of her shoebox, bit him squarely on his toe and dashed back to safety. That was the one and only time she ever bit anyone. From the sound of her evil chuckle, she was very pleased she had.

This was 13 years ago and I still laugh when I think about it.

Jo Rhoze
Bundaberg, Queensland
Australia

Is this too much affection?

Being very affectionate is one thing, but I think I am being taken advantage of by my female cockatiel called Pablo.

When she spends time with me perched on my finger she will begin to make a kissing noise, tap her beak on my hand, give me a wolf whistle and fan out her tail feathers. Then she bears down and rubs her 'vent' on whatever part of my hand she can reach. I am not sure, but I don't think she is 'itchy' but is going through some courting ritual with me! She does not engage in this behavior with my husband, only me, and insists on a kiss when she is finished!

Is this perverted or normal for a cockatiel with an identity crisis?

Can you offer any advice? Contact us at SMARTER than JACK.

6

Smart animals find solutions

A novel solution

One day I noticed a fox picking tufts of wool off the wire fence in a few different places. She ended up with a small ball of wool, which she carried in her mouth. The wool was from sheep that had jumped through the wire of the fence.

The fox then trotted down to the Mortlock River and backed into the water. She gradually kept backing deeper into the water until all the water was above her mouth and nose and the ball of wool. Then she let the wool go and it floated away.

I grabbed the wool a little way down from where the fox had let it go and noticed that it was full of fleas.

Frank Watson
Singleton
Western Australia

Lamb care center

One week, I noticed each morning when I was leaving for work that our six lambs would be all together in the driveway. They were in the care of two of the ewes, while the other ewes were over on the grass stuffing their faces. Nothing unusual in that really, except I observed that each day there were two different ewes with them – they seemed

to be working a lamb-minding roster as they all took a turn while the others were free to graze. After they had all taken a turn the first ones came back on duty, and they worked through the roster again.

How did they know who was on duty? Who organized this system? It just goes to show that sheep are not really stupid at all. Not kindergarten but lambergarten.

We have one young ewe who used to leap about like a springbok when she was a lamb, and now I see that her lamb is just the same. She stood staring at me for a moment, then took off leaping with her front legs tucked against her chest as she sprang forward. It really looks quite hilarious.

With such a small flock of sheep we have come to know each of them as individuals, and it really is quite enlightening to realize that sheep are just like any other living creature, with their likes and dislikes, their friends and enemies, and their individual characteristics and habits that are not so obvious when farming large flocks of several hundred sheep.

Adrian Holloway
Palmerston North
New Zealand

Time to go ashore

Our friends Jim and Cynthia take their Border collie Ned when they go out in their yacht. Early on he developed an ingenious method of telling them he wanted to be taken ashore.

Unless Ned wanted to swim, he knew the dinghy was his only mode of transport. The problem was that the little boat floated several meters away at the end of its painter, which was tied to the stern of the yacht. How was he to bring it within jumping range?

Ned at sea

At first he tried pulling on the painter, but the dinghy didn't come close enough before falling back to its original position. He overcame this problem by grabbing the rope further out, while it was still slack from his initial pull, and tugging it again.

After he'd repeated this procedure several times, the dinghy was much closer. He had also pulled in a loop of rope long enough to allow him to walk along the deck with it in his mouth. With a little trial and error he had the right-sized loop for the dinghy to come

right in and bump against the stern. At this point he abandoned the rope and ran back aft to jump in before it slipped away.

Finally, from his position in the dinghy, he could lock his eyes on Jim's – and the message was loud and clear. *Okay, now we go ashore!*

Wendy Willett
Queensland
Australia

What happened there?

I had been happily entertained in the garden by the antics of squirrels chasing each other. One of them sat at the edge of the narrow garden path, intently eating one of the nuts I fed to them each time. It sat upright, its bushy tail over its head. Suddenly I froze.

A neighbor's cat had appeared, edging stealthily toward the squirrel. Should I rush out and scatter them? I poised, ready for action, but decided to wait a few more seconds to see what nature intended. The two creatures faced each other, the squirrel seemingly unconcerned, the cat crouching, ready to pounce. I was amazed by what followed.

The second the cat launched itself, the squirrel simply jumped over the cat and landed on the ground again, still concentrating on eating the nut. The cat looked around in sheer disbelief, shook itself and slunk away.

Mrs Stella Palmer
Sheffield
England

Speak English, please!

We have friends who have an assortment of Australian parrots, among them a sulphur-crested cockatoo with a large vocabulary. His owners claim he can talk for half an hour without repeating himself.

We have often taken visitors to their farm to see the birds, and one day took two people from Germany. Unfortunately the cockatoo was saying nothing, and all our coaxing was to no avail.

The two young German men were standing in front of his cage and speaking to each other in German. After a few minutes the cockatoo turned his head to one side and said, *What did you say?* Naturally, we all broke up laughing.

Charles Walker
Heyfield, Victoria
Australia

Useful tool

One day I observed a butcher-bird catch a mouse.

Then he had a problem: he couldn't tear it apart as he had no way of holding it. After trying for a while, he saw something that would do the trick. He poked the mouse through a link in a chain that was holding some machinery in place.

With the mouse held firmly in the link, he was able to enjoy his meal!

Vashti Grubb
Monto, Queensland
Australia

Write to me ...
Vashti Grubb
20 Wheatley Street
Monto QLD 4630
AUSTRALIA

The baby-snatcher

Missy was broody – she wanted nothing more than babies of her own. Here she was, a young fit German shepherd in the prime of her life, and her owners had made it impossible for her to breed.

Not to be outdone, she went scouting around the neighborhood for unattended little ones. At first her new babies were kittens carried home gently in her mouth to her kennel, where she would proceed to contentedly groom them. Of course, her embarrassed owners would then have to ask around the neighbors as to where to find the original mother so that the snaffled ones could be safely returned.

Later she graduated to puppies, and yet again the hunt was on so that they could be reinstated in their original homes.

Thwarted she was not, as one day I looked out the dining room window and there was Missy guiding with her nose a real live human baby just at the toddling stage. Gently, she was nudging him down the long driveway toward her kennel. Neither baby nor dog thought this particularly unusual – it was me that was about to have kittens. My dog, the baby-snatcher! I could just see the headlines. Duly, the baby was returned to the original owner, with no ill effects to the baby or myself.

Realizing we had to do something to stop this aberrant behavior – and fortunately we were about to shift towns – we legally acquired for her a real puppy to guide into adulthood, which thankfully satisfied her completely.

Glenis Allan
Auckland
New Zealand

Write to me ...
email Glenis
jeff.allan@xtra.co.nz

Mother's first lesson

Raccoons, bears and even coyotes are smart enough to have learned that houses and humans mean food. One deer knew they also meant safety.

The morning air was bright on the mountains behind my house, when the neighbors' dogs started barking. It wasn't their normal bark – they were frantic. They weren't out front, so it couldn't be a stranger at the door. I lifted the kitchen curtain and peered out.

A deer stood in my backyard, something obviously wrong. She was panting and pacing, almost staggering. Sweat glistened on her flanks and her mouth gaped with each breath. The whites of her eyes bulged.

I wasn't sure what to do. Animal Control would put her down without getting near enough to find out what was wrong. I didn't want to risk her life if I didn't have to. She might have eaten the wrong thing, and after throwing it up she'd be fine. I waited. But within minutes a flood of liquid from her hindquarters told me what was really happening: she was giving birth.

I called next door to get them to take their dogs in. My backyard was surrounded by a high fence, but she didn't need the stress from their yapping.

I watched as she gave birth to first one, then a second baby deer. She cleaned them up and, once they'd tottered to their feet, let them have their first drink of her milk. Then she nudged them into hiding, one under a bush and the other on the opposite side of the yard, tucked under the edge of my deck. If I hadn't known they were there I would have missed them. Their coats blended with the dappled shadows, camouflaging them entirely.

Surprisingly, the mother started to leave. The fawn under the bush struggled to his feet to follow her. But the doe turned back, and

pushed him firmly back into place. The message was obvious: *Stay here!* Then she left.

I waited all day for her to come back. She didn't. Predators would be attracted by the smell of new life so she had to be hiding the fawns, but surely they couldn't go all day without her? Not on their first day in the world.

She still hadn't returned by nightfall. When I looked out, I turned on the back-door light and saw one small ear flicker. They were still there. I decided that if she hadn't returned by morning I'd call Animal Control. Without food for that long, they'd die.

The next morning they were still there. I sighed. Something must have happened to the mother, or she'd forgotten where she'd left them. But, even as I reached for the phone, like sunlight she walked back into my yard. She picked her way carefully to one baby, then to the other, letting them both drink before they left. The last I saw of her, she was slowly striding down our street, the two tiny fawns at her heels as she proudly led them out of town.

Her leaving them for the night had been their first lesson: where and how to hide. She'd also taught them that a human's fenced-in backyard is the safest hiding place of all.

Sharman Horwood
Seoul
South Korea

Write to me ...
email Sharman
sharmanh2004@yahoo.ca

Sharman Horwood is a Canadian writer living in Seoul, South Korea.

The midnight marauder

Over the course of our married life we've owned a number of homes, all of which we've 'adjusted' to a greater or lesser extent in order to meet our own particular tastes.

So it didn't seem such a momentous decision to embark on yet another house renovation to occupy us in our retirement years. The house we chose to purchase was middle-aged, and in need of a major cleaning and a significant amount of upgrading and modernization. Perhaps its one difference was the fact that it was on the outskirts of a village rather than a city. Located 35 minutes from the nearest major town, it came complete with large oak trees, nearby meadows and rivers, and wildlife. This was to be our new environment.

We quickly realized that squirrels and chipmunks had also staked a claim to our property. The lawn was pockmarked with holes – perfectly round and located in strategic spots that allowed fleeing chipmunks a quick getaway. Many of the holes were close together, perhaps housing chipmunk condominiums. Some of these communities were active, others dormant. One of the most active areas was in the middle of my flower garden. Watching what few flowers we had disappear as a new entrance or exit appeared was beginning to aggravate me. My joy in watching the antics of these hyperactive rodents started to wane.

However, gardening would have to wait. Cleaning the house came first, which necessitated the use of a variety of agents purporting to remove almost every type of dirt and grime. Of course, they neglected to add that the most important additive to my cleaning arsenal was elbow grease.

Notwithstanding our new-found aches and pains, we were gradually gaining ground and felt rather pleased with ourselves. The kitchen presented the biggest challenge, especially when we realized we had another rodent problem. At least, we assumed this was the

reason for the tiny oval-shaped droppings we found in various parts of the kitchen. Most seemed to be located behind the clothes dryer, but in spite of our efforts to seal the hose to the dryer we were unsuccessful in discouraging our midnight marauder. The intruder also seemed impervious to our potions, although each night, with great care, I provided poison and water in mouse-sized containers.

Recognizing that the problem lay in the dryer ventilation system, my husband donned knee pads, took a trouble-light and modern dryer ventilation tubing, and descended into the crawl space. Several exhausting hours later, he declared us to be sealed tight. No critter would be able to enter our stronghold.

Next came the important task of attaching the new hose to the dryer. In order to make adaptations to the new system, we needed to turn and tip the dryer on its side. Something inside rattled. It was a new and very strange sound. We confronted the dryer and began to dismantle it.

We removed the top. Everything looked normal. Then the back panel. Nothing appeared out of place. Next came the plate at the back of the control panel, containing the electrical wiring and switches.

To our amazement, out poured hundreds of miniature dog food pellets. Mesmerized by the torrent, we were astonished to see them falling from perfectly stacked columns that would have withstood the scrutiny of any warehouse superintendent. Each pellet of dog food, interspersed with the occasional small dog bone biscuit, was neatly packed in and around the wiring. It was beautifully done and precisely organized, and probably contained a year's supply of what we could only guess must be chipmunk food.

We were dumbfounded, unable to assimilate the ingenuity of our miniature entrepreneur. Clearly our unwelcome visitor had discovered a warm, dry and accessible pantry, with a limitless supply of food. But where did he get it?

It was a minute or two before we remembered the configuration of the family that had so recently vacated these premises. They were an older couple who, because of poor health, had been forced to relocate near their children. Food and water dishes for their chihuahua had been placed beside the dryer.

Our enterprising chipmunk, entering through the broken outside vent and torn hose, must have found this daily supply of food and gone about the business of storing it for future use, carrying each load up the electrical wiring into the 5 by 28 inch space that housed the control panel. How long this had been going on was a mystery, and we were surprised there had not been an electrical fire. We can only conclude that our smart friend had conducted his business at

An enterprising chipmunk

night, slipping in and out without the knowledge of their family and perhaps their dog as well.

As for the wee dog, further questions remain. Did he go hungry as his food disappeared with unrelenting frequency? Did he graciously watch while his guest ate his dinner? Did dog and chipmunk play while humans slept? The mind races as different scenarios present themselves. One can only hope that at least the dog was praised for his very healthy appetite.

Vivian Collver
Marmora, Ontario
Canada

A goat with a head for heights

While sailing in New Caledonia, we moored beneath a cliff near the entrance to a river in fairly remote countryside.

We observed three goats on the rocky shore as they went about their business among the boulders, rubble and shale of their habitat at the base of the cliff. Their domain would have been no more than ten feet wide and about a quarter of a mile long, bordered by the harbor on one side and a vertical cliff on the other. I was mesmerized by their agility: their hooves seemed to cling to the rocks as if by suction cups.

I watched as one goat trotted effortlessly to the top of a large vertical pyramid-shaped rock some 15 feet off the ground. Just as I was admiring his sure-footed arrival at the top, he stood on his hind legs on the point of the rock and pawed at an out-of-reach branch.

He managed to grab it and eat from it – still balanced on his hind legs. He maintained this stance for some minutes, only coming back down onto all fours once he'd stripped the branch. He was not only sure-footed and agile but extremely dexterous too.

I couldn't help but wonder what these amazing creatures did at night. Visions of them sitting around knitting cashmere jumpers did not seem unrealistic.

Terri Aufmanis
Fairlight, New South Wales
Australia

Your say . . .

Here at SMARTER than JACK we love reading the mail we receive from people who have been involved with our books. This mail includes letters both from contributors and readers and from the animal welfare charities that have benefited. We thought we would share with you excerpts from some of the letters that really touched our hearts.

'Thank you for including our dear Jess in your publication. We are very pleased that, in this way, Jessie will live on in the hearts of many.'

Sandy, Canada

'We are thrilled to be part of this terrific program, SMARTER than JACK. Creator Jenny Campbell has hit on a wonderful combination of producing heart-warming books of animal stories with a revenue program to help animal welfare organizations. It's fun, easy and doesn't require a large time commitment from us to make it work. We are very grateful for the opportunity to work with Jenny and her team and we highly recommend that other animal welfare groups do the same.'

Sheelagh MacDonald, Programs Director
Canadian Federation of Humane Societies

'I am thrilled Tonia's story is reaching a wider audience and will help raise money for other disadvantaged animals.'

Julie, Australia

'I would like to say thank you for all the wonderful stories. They are great and they always keep me interested to the last word!'

Clare

'We are thrilled to join forces with such an innovative and exciting program. Not only do the books themselves entertain and inspire with stories that will make people see animals for the unique, intelligent creatures they are, but the money that can be raised by selling the books can help improve the lives of so many animals in need. Nothing is smarter than that!'

Jennie Taylor Martin, Director of Customer Service, Merchandise, Literature
PETA Foundation

'Dear Lisa, I am utterly thrilled to receive your news.

Dear Coco died in 2002 and my precious mate Milo died last January. I was heartbroken and resolved never to get another dog as it was just too hard to lose him. However, you renewed my confidence and I have brought home from the RSPCA two delightful dogs whose owner had died. One is a Cavalier King Charles spaniel, Katie, and the other is a black miniature schnauzer, Jesse. So we are off on a new adventure.'

June, Australia

'What a fantastic way to celebrate the spirit and splendor of the animals in our lives ... you have really captured the magnificence of our animal friends.'

Heather Irving, Executive Director
P.E.I. Humane Society

'Jenny – I was informed that the book SMARTER than JACK was in my mail when I was away so needless to say I could not wait to get home and open it. When I did open it to Kody's story I had a reaction like I have never had before – a big smile of pride, and tears of sadness rolling down my cheeks for my best friend – I did not know whether to laugh or cry – in the end I did both 'cause there was Kody's picture and story for everyone to see and read.

Thank you so very much – I cannot tell you how much I appreciate what you have done for me. Your book has fulfilled my wish to tell everyone (the world) what a great guy Kody was, how so very special he was as my buddy. Hard even for me to believe but I am still very greatly affected at my loss, of his not being with me. I plan to purchase and send some books to my friends and to the veterinarians who cared for Kody.'

Stan, Canada

Lisa and Anthea of SMARTER than JACK enjoy some letters

7

Smart animals have fun

Channel surfing

One of my favorite cat stories involves our now-deceased Sphynx, Ra. It was no secret that Ra was extremely intelligent and observant. He liked to watch our daily routines, and made a habit of watching everything we did with great interest.

My husband Jeff had come home on his lunch break one day and was watching TV. He left the remote control lying on the seat of the couch when he went back to work. That evening I came home to find the TV turned on. The Animal Planet channel was on. Both our cats, Zuki and Ra, were sound asleep in their beds and looked like they hadn't stirred all day. I knew better, though.

When Jeff arrived home from work later, I asked him why he had left the TV on and why he was watching Animal Planet, as he rarely watches that channel. He replied that, although he had been watching TV, it was the ABC channel and he had turned the TV off before he left to go back to work.

It didn't take long to piece the story together from there. Ra had managed to turn the TV on with the remote, and even changed it to a channel with animals. We assume he did this by sitting or jumping on the buttons on the remote, but who knows. He was a very observant and intelligent cat, and always enjoyed watching TV with us in the evenings.

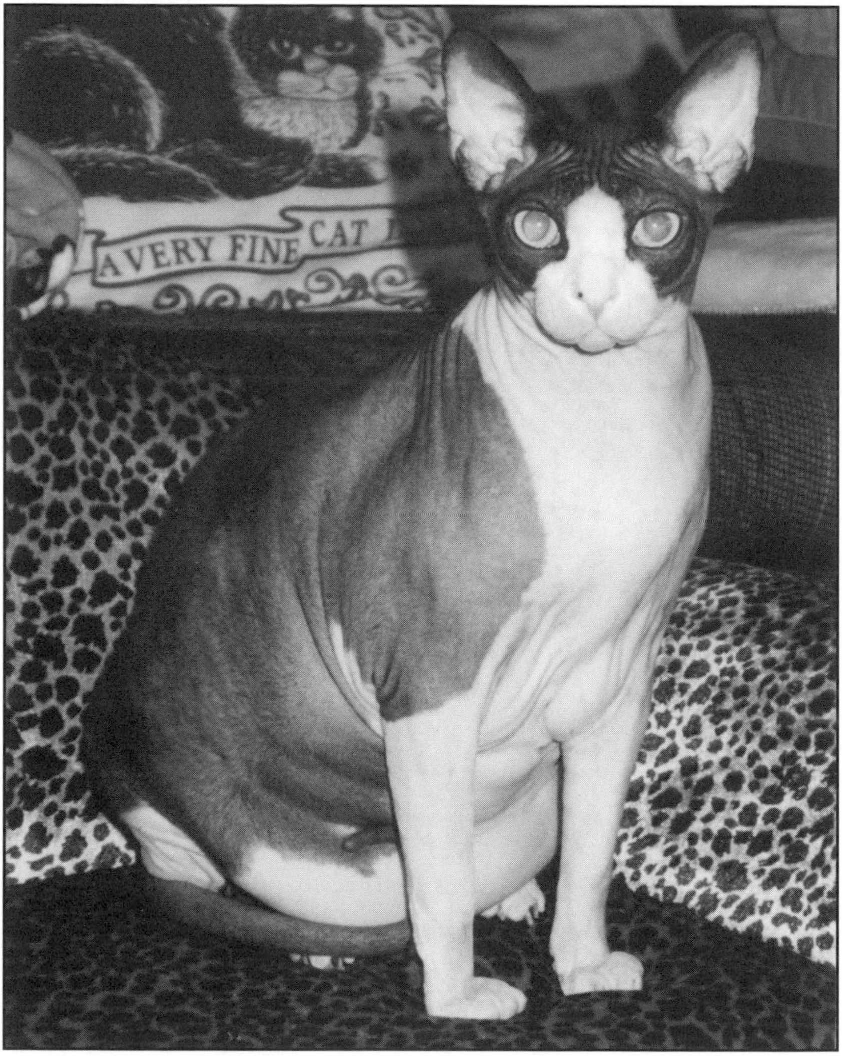

Did Ra choose to watch the Animal Planet channel?

We wonder to this day, did he watch TV often while we were at work, and perhaps just forget to turn the TV off that day before I got home? Had he watched us use the remote so often that he figured out to operate it? We will never know.

But one thing is for sure – Ra thought TV was quite entertaining, and he especially liked animal and bird shows.

Kathy and Jeff Hoffman
Kearney, Nebraska
United States

Spectators

I went up to Yulong Park at Medowie, which is not far from Williamstown Air Force Base, to watch my grandson play soccer. As I settled on the sideline I looked up to the far end of the ground and saw three large kangaroos hopping around. As the game progressed I noticed that the kangaroos had stood erect and were looking at the game. They continued watching till the game had finished.

As I was folding my chair I looked across to the other side of the ground. The three kangaroos were hopping very fast down to the bottom of the ground. I thought they were heading toward some bush that was there. But I was wrong. There was a game of soccer going on between six- and seven-year-olds. I couldn't believe what I saw. The three kangaroos had stopped hopping and, standing erect side by side, were watching the game.

The locals didn't take any notice of the kangaroos, so I thought they must be regulars.

I can verify this by getting statements from the parents and the boys who played in the team on the day. At my local bowls club I

told them about the actions of the kangaroos and one bright wag wanted to know if they were waving the Aussie flag!

Arthur Hiskens
Cardiff, New South Wales
Australia

Write to me ...
Arthur Hiskens
c/- Smarter than Jack
PO Box 27003
Wellington
NEW ZEALAND

The worldwide horse/goat alliance

I have lived in the country most of my life and spend a great deal of time communing with nature. I watch animals interact with their environment, humans and each other, and I've noticed some rather odd things.

Take, for example, the curious alliance between horses and goats. In case you haven't noticed, horses are deeply attached to goats – and vice versa.

I used to commute 64 miles round trip to work every day. Driving down the narrow, twisty country road into town, I would pass a small fenced-in pasture where lived a golden-colored horse and a white billy goat.

It struck me that the goat and the horse were always in close proximity, much closer than a couple of acres of wandering room would normally require. In fact, most of the time they were head-to-head.

One morning as I passed by, it looked as though the goat was reading the riot act to his equine buddy. They were facing each other and the goat's mouth was open wide, his lower jaw working from side to side as though he was yelling at the horse.

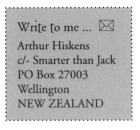

Just before I rounded the bend and the pair passed from view, I saw the horse raise a front leg over the goat's head, then bring his hoof down once, sharply, hitting the goat smack dab in the middle of his forehead. I could almost hear him say, *Aw, shut up!* I laughed all the way to work that day, and still smile – just as I'm doing right now – whenever I think of it.

On other occasions, I noticed that the goat – who had escaped from the field they both shared – was grazing on the tall weeds just outside the fence's perimeter. Never far from his buddy, the horse was there too, grazing just on the other side of the fence.

One morning I met both of them parading toward me in the middle of my traffic lane on the two-lane road. The goat was in the lead. As he ambled hesitantly behind, the horse's demeanor was the reverse of his strutting friend. With his head down, and glancing warily from side to side, the horse appeared to say, *You've done it now, Goat. We're going to be in such trouble when they catch us out here.*

Since then, I've noticed other horse/goat alliances in many different places in the world. It appears to me as though a special affection exists between these two species. Perhaps it's due to their thousands of years of shared history in man's barnyards and fields. I don't know. I only know that they seem to have a very close relationship.

Jean C Fisher
Sebastopol, California
United States

Dare to be different

Every day as I clean my teeth I watch our current St Andrews Cross spider living her life on the outside of our bathroom window.

Over a period of 14 months several of these spiders have occupied this area, obviously a prime piece of real estate for them. We have spied on their mating and delighted in the resulting nursery of littlies

which, despite our concerns of being overrun, have all left to seek their fortunes elsewhere. Even their mum left and, despite feeling bereft, we grabbed the chance to clean the window. Now we again find ourselves playing host to a single spider and things are back to normal – or are they?

All webs, until recently, have been the usual cross fanning out from the four groups of legs. Even the youngsters made a very creditable effort at conforming to the regulation shape. When wind threatens, the webs are thickened up, often before it arrives. Sometimes just two of the radials are thickened, but strong or gale force winds always require the strengthening of all four. As this thickening occasionally occurs when the wind doesn't get up, we suspect that they – like the Weather Bureau – are not infallible.

Our current St Andrews Cross spider is not your common or garden character, though. She does not like to conform, and displays her individuality in her web. The radials are usually of unequal length and angle, and frequently crooked. Sometimes only one or two show up, for she is quite frugal with her thread. Last week three radials were tiny, and the fourth was extra long and wavering as if she had an urge to make curves. Imagine being born into a body that must always produce straight lines! As a lover of curves myself, I could appreciate the temptation.

The chore of teeth cleaning has become, for me as a struggling nonconformist, a time of encouragement and inspiration as I watch our intrepid little spider expressing her individuality. She doesn't concern herself with how others see her, but just does what comes naturally to her, not her species. Vive la différence!

Wendy Willett
Russell Island, Queensland
Australia

A rabbit who played with toy cars

When my family was living in Victoria, Britsh Columbia about 30 years ago, a friend asked my son Brian to choose a baby rabbit from a litter. Junior, as he named the black and white Dutch rabbit, quickly became a loved pet.

One Saturday afternoon Brian hid him in a carryall bag and sneaked him onto the Victoria Transit. He took the rabbit to a local fair and Junior came home with a blue ribbon. We were elated.

We were transferred to Toronto in 1973. Junior traveled in a regulation crate placed in the hold of the plane, but the captain personally assured Brian that all was well, and we all arrived safely.

Junior would join in when my sons played with their Dinky cars on the patio. They would line the cars up, and Junior would go to the blue one and pick it up with his mouth, then throw it as far as he could. He repeated this over and over, and the blue car was his favorite.

Brian sometimes relaxed on a canvas-covered lounge chair. Junior didn't like him resting and would go under the chair and try to push him with his head. He'd eventually end up lying across Brian's chest, fast asleep.

He loved raisins, and when Brian put a small box down for him he would persevere until he opened it up so that he could scoff the contents. This was usually on a Saturday evening when Brian watched hockey on TV. Junior would sneak under his jacket and they'd enjoy the game together.

Brian is now married with two children of his own. They live in the country and his children chose a rabbit for their pet.

Catherine Goldie
Mississauga, Ontario
Canada

Doggy dumb-bell

A friend had bought Clancy and Keira a doggy dumb-bell for their Christmas present. The dumb-bell, when they carried it around, would make different noises. Both dogs loved it very much.

Clancy is usually a very good-natured dog and is happy to share his toys and food with Keira. That all changed when the doggy dumb-bell was presented to them on Christmas Day. There would be no sharing of this toy and Clancy claimed it for his own. If Keira even went close to the toy he would immediately snatch it up, snarl at her, then put it next to him or sleep on it. If Keira should be lucky enough to get hold of the dumb-bell, Clancy would chase her until she dropped it or he would take it directly out of her mouth.

This particular day, Clancy was sleeping on the lounge with his head resting on the bar of the dumb-bell and Keira was asleep on the other side of the lounge. Clancy woke up and needed to answer the call of nature. He got up off the lounge and, after checking that Keira was still asleep, proceeded to go outside to do his business. As soon as Keira heard the dog door flap, indicating that Clancy was outside, she ran over to the dumb-bell, grabbed it, ran into our bedroom and put it under the bed, then ran back to her spot on the lounge, lay back down and pretended to be asleep.

Clancy came back inside and straight away noticed the dumb-bell was missing. He went to Keira and started pushing at her with his nose; she still pretended to be asleep! He pushed her a bit more with his nose and was trying to look underneath her when she slowly opened her eyes, stood up, gave a big stretch and looked at Clancy like she was saying *What?*

Clancy then did a big search of the lounge room, including under the cushions and behind the lounge. Keira quietly looked on, and then proceeded to entice Clancy into a game and he forgot about the missing dumb-bell.

When we went to bed that night Keira wanted to sleep under our bed instead of on her own bed. Clancy went to his bed and proceeded to go to sleep, until he heard the noise of the dumb-bell coming from under our bed. The chase was on again.

Cathy Gillot
Worrigee, New South Wales
Australia

The useful cat flap

Our late basset hound Longfellow Mademoiselle Melina (known to her friends as Cujo) was a couch potato but no mental slouch. She showed this one day when she wasn't allowed inside with her favorite toy, a monkey which had a habit of shedding its stuffing.

My wife Raewyn was hosting a meeting of fellow teachers at our home that afternoon so had everything spotless before she went to work. That meant Cujo, who was standing at the back door and scratching to be let in, was repeatedly told that she could not come inside with the monkey, which she had in her mouth.

Eventually, answering the umpteenth scratch, Raewyn – seeing that the monkey had disappeared – opened the door and let Cujo in. She fairly flew inside, then sprinted to the cat flap (which she could only get her nose through) on the other side of the house where she had deposited the monkey, snatched it up and charged across the living room, liberally sprinkling stuffing all the way.

Peter Jackson
Kaitaia
New Zealand

Write to me ...
email Peter
editor@northnz.co.nz

Even crows have fun

I woke up early one morning to a scratching sound. The sound went away so I drifted back to sleep.

A few minutes later I woke to the same sound. This time it persisted. I decided I should get up and find out where it was coming from.

My house isn't very big. Just a modular home on a nicely treed lot in Kitimat, British Columbia. I had seen many animals walk, trot, climb, gallop or waddle across the yard, but I'd never seen what I witnessed that bright spring morning in 2003.

In the kitchen, I heard the noise above me. I looked up to the ceiling, to see a crow step on the upper edge of the high-impact plastic skylight. It did a little sidestepping and then slid down the plastic skylight. To my amazement, there were two other crows doing the same thing.

The first would go down the 'slide', walk back up and wait its turn. This went on for about five minutes, until one looked down with a sideways glare. They'd seen me watching. With one caw they were gone.

Daniel Carter
Kitimat, British Columbia
Canada

Write to me ... ✉
email Daniel
dartcart@telus.net

Mighty mouse

I woke one night to say to my wife, 'Did you hear that?'

The sound was similar to that made by our pet white mouse Woody when running on the treadmill in his cage. He had died and, as my daughter had gone off to university around the same time, the cage was stored in her empty bedroom.

My wife told me that I was dreaming and to go to sleep. A little later that night I heard it again. I ran downstairs, convinced I wasn't dreaming. Yet when I turned on the light in the downstairs bedroom – nothing. I checked the cage and still nothing.

We talked about it the next day and my wife told me I was dreaming. I thought perhaps she was right.

The next night I heard it again and, after my swift move downstairs with the torch, still nothing. This wasn't going to beat me. So I slept in the spare bedroom, where the cage was, because I was sure it came from the cage. I had my trusty torch at the ready.

About an hour later, yet again I heard the sound. It was definitely the treadmill. Without a sound I pointed the torch at the cage and turned it on. There to my amazement I saw a little brown field mouse running on the treadmill. When he saw the light he promptly vacated the exercise equipment, squeezed himself through the bars of the cage and hid in the wardrobe.

Now, our Woody took a week to learn the knack of the treadmill and never tried to squeeze out through the bars. We thought this little mighty mouse deserved to live, and for a week or so after that we would hear the treadmill going on and off most nights.

We never really knew what happened to him after that. Perhaps the novelty of the treadmill wore off and he went on some other adventure.

Andrew and Susan Gawlik
Rotorua
New Zealand

A dog on wheels

Pumpkin, our black Labrador, is mad about skateboarding.

She loves it so much that once, when a young boy and his friend were skating down the road, she ran out, jumped on their skateboard

and left a surprised and bemused skater behind while she pushed off and went rolling into the sunset. We have to keep her own skateboard hidden in the shed, because as soon as she sees it she starts to bark and whine and won't leave us alone until she's had a ride.

She places two front paws on the board and pushes with her two back legs. She has even made it to having three legs on and pushing with one. What happens when she crashes, you may ask? Well, she is so smart that she has taught herself how to flip the board back onto its wheels if it turns over, and then she's off again. A couple of years ago at sports day, Pumpkin skated the length of the school oval, with a cheering crowd of parents and children. Ever since, she has made a regular appearance each year.

Artemis Wilkinson
Victoria
Australia

Cat tricks

Milo the shih-tzu was running from the back door to the front window, keeping his eye on someone in the street. Coco the cat was lying just off his pathway.

After about the sixth time Milo ran past her, Coco put out her leg and tripped him up.

June Green
Melbourne, Victoria
Australia

Write to me ...
email June
jgre3549@bigpond.net.au

8

Smart animals make us wonder

Trixie's last good-bye

I was sitting on the back steps enjoying a mug of coffee in the early spring sunshine, when I became aware of someone or something trying to capture my attention. It was Trixie, our ancient 16-human-years-old grey tabby cat. Poor old Trixie was a rather plain old puss, with no apparent redeeming features other than her constant affection.

She was just sitting on the wet concrete path staring at me as if in a trance. I looked into her tired old yellow eyes, and she stared back at me without a blink as if willing me to pick her up. It was all rather surreal. I felt obliged to talk to her and she responded by making a painful effort to get onto my lap. I duly patted and cuddled her, thinking, 'How bony you are, Trix.' She relaxed on my lap for a wee while. I gave her a kiss on the head and, with as strong an effort as she could muster, she very purposefully left my lap and headed for the shed with a strength that I had not witnessed for some time.

I had a foreboding about her behavior, so I went to investigate why the almost sprightly walk to the shed. And there she was, on an old rug, quite dead.

She had obviously sensed that her time on earth was at a close. Needless to say, I shed quite a few tears at the shock of finding her like that within minutes of her being in my company.

On reflection, I feel quite humbled that she chose to spend her last moments on my lap as a final parting.

We miss you, Trix.

June Spragg
Auckland
New Zealand

Trixie said good-bye

He found himself a mate … and he chose me!

A young male pigeon landed on my neighbor's parked car one day during the spring of 2002.

We noticed that when cats stalked him he didn't fly away. A closer inspection revealed that one wing was injured and a nail on his right claw was missing. We fed him birdseed, gave him water and hoped he'd be able to survive, as there were many cats in the neighborhood. I started to talk to him, and mimic his call and actions. That was the beginning of our strange relationship. I called him Burd.

His wing healed quickly but he continued to stay with us. As winter approached I became concerned for his well-being, so provided a small outdoor shelter for him. Not only was he free to come and go as he pleased, I was hoping he would find a mate.

Instead, I think I became his mate. He started to follow me around the house, flying to each windowsill to watch me from outside. He'd try to get my attention when I gardened, and would follow me down the street when I took the dogs for a walk. Sometimes he'd even stand on my head during the walk. It was hard for him to balance but he tried to go as far as he could before he flew home.

He would sit on the peaks of our neighbors' homes and wait until he saw me, when he'd either try to land on my head again for the walk home or simply swoop around me. It was commonplace for him to be on my head while I visited and talked with neighbors.

He would land on top of the car when I drove up the street on my way home, stand on it while I drove away … and eventually fly home. When I sat out on the deck he would coo and dance along the rail, around my head. If anyone else sat on that chair, he would peck them and hit them with his wing.

At first it was funny, but he could be quite aggressive. He seemed to feel he had to protect me; I was his mate. I stopped getting the newspaper, as every time the delivery person approached the house

she was attacked by Burd. When I tried to make other arrangements to receive my paper, they wanted to write a story and take photos of him, and our story made the front page.

Burd would come to the front window with twigs in his mouth for me. He'd tap on the window, jump onto the front stoop and wait to be let into the house. Once inside, he would go direct to the closet and place the twig down. When I let him back outside, he'd repeat the process. I finally realized that he wanted me to build a nest.

As winter of 2003 approached, I noticed a hawk in the neighborhood. I was concerned, as hawks are used to control the pigeon population.

I'd often see the hawk chasing Burd, and it was always a relief when he returned safely home. After repeatedly seeing him fly away with the hawk on his tail, it was obvious that the hawk was determined to rid the neighborhood of this pigeon. And one day Burd didn't come home. Friends and neighbors waited anxiously for news of his return but to no avail. Did the hawk get him, or was he able to fly to a safe place? I feared the worst, and I really missed him. He was part of our family.

While walking the dogs during the fall of 2004 I saw a group of pigeons, including one that looked a lot like Burd. When I approached them, all but one flew away. My heart skipped a beat. He acted a little cautious, but was obviously intrigued by us and the dogs. I wanted to see if he was missing a nail on his right claw, but wasn't able to get that close.

He danced around, cooed and then flew away to the rest of the flock. I still have a smile on my face.

Sharon Sora
Etobicoke, Ontario
Canada

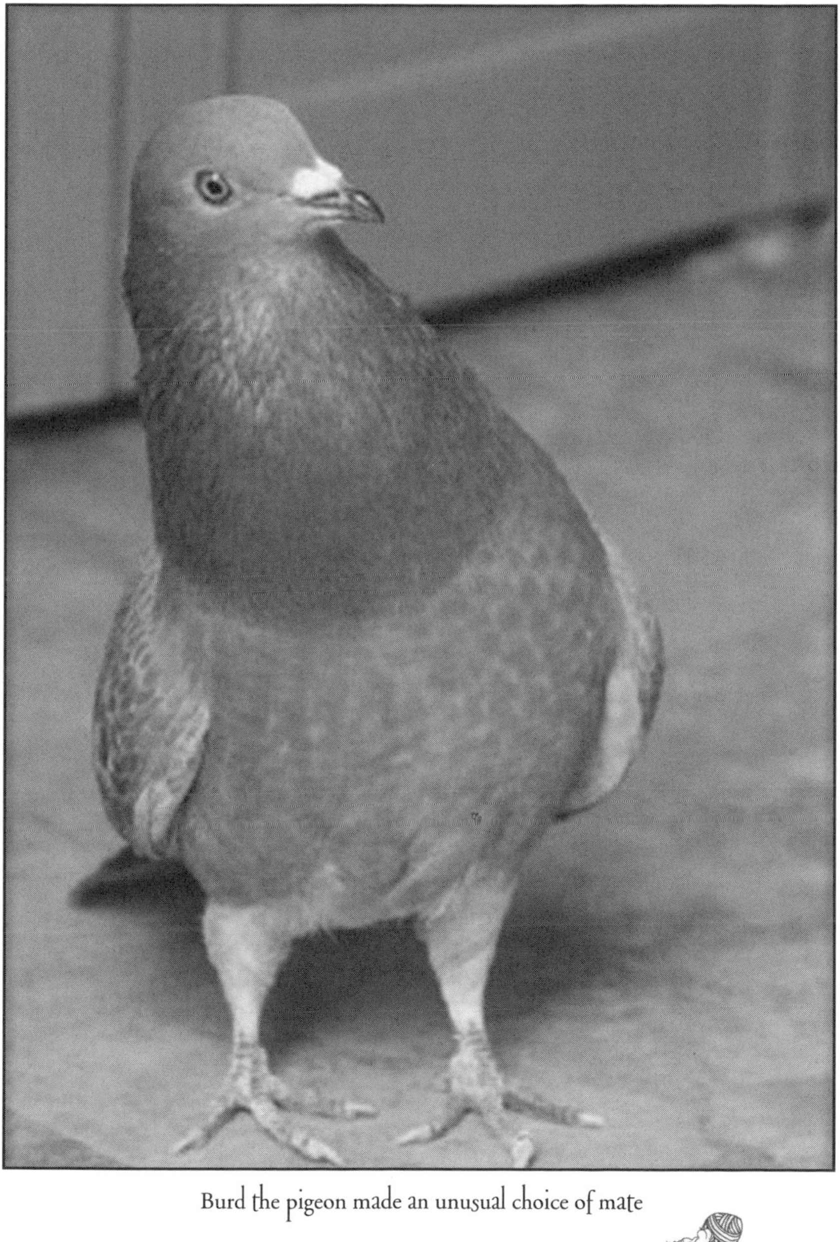

Burd the pigeon made an unusual choice of mate

Saved by a smelly stranger

It was a breathlessly hot February night and I lay in bed in my flat in Melbourne, Australia wishing I were dead. Marriage to a fellow New Zealander, which had taken place in a moment of youthful madness three years earlier and been in trouble practically ever since, had finally blown apart. That evening, after a tremendous argument, my husband had stormed out of the flat, vowing never to return.

Now, alone and distraught, I was experiencing the bitter taste of disappointment and defeat. I had tried my hardest. I had failed. My life was over. If only, I said to myself, that could literally be true. If only I could close my eyes and never wake up again. If only God would give me a heart attack. Or a fatal stroke.

Problems always loom larger at night. My thoughts got wilder and wilder. I forgot about my interesting job on a local television station. I forgot about my many Melbourne friends. Nothing mattered anymore. All I wanted to do was die.

Suddenly there was a sound at the window. A scraping, scratching sound. Under normal circumstances I would have been paralyzed with fright, but now that sound drifted over me. So what if it were a burglar. Let him come and take what he wanted. A fat lot I cared! The scraping turned into a thump – or rather a double thump – as something landed on the polished wooden floor. Then came a pattering sound, followed by my own gasp of surprise as the intruder landed on my chest.

I had seen the cat a number of times before. He was a whisker-thin chocolate point Siamese with glorious, if rather squinty, blue eyes and a loud, insistent cry. His owners, who must have lived nearby, obviously took little interest in him beyond supplying the daily rations. Or perhaps they had tried and given up.

For the Siamese had one extremely offensive habit. He was an oil freak. He liked nothing better than to roll in the oil on the concrete under parked cars. My husband's pride and joy, although a prestige model, was distinctly old and it dripped oil. I had sometimes seen the cat under the car, flat on his back, legs in the air, wriggling about in apparent ecstasy.

As a result he always looked grubby. And he smelled dreadful. On several occasions he had invited himself inside the flat but his visits had always been brief. He had marched from room to room, examining this and that, with the air of a landlord making a formal inspection. But never before had he entered at night. Now, however, he settled himself on top of me and began purring. Like his meow – if the harsh, wailing sound he made could be described as such – his purr was considerably louder than that of the more down-market of his species to which I had been accustomed. He purred and purred.

'Oh, you smelly old thing,' I blubbed, stroking his oily back.

The Siamese edged himself further up my chest until his head nestled by the side of my neck. Then he lay still. He purred. I stroked. And, gradually, with the rhythm of the purring and stroking and the comforting feel of the warm, throbbing body, the knot of despair in my chest subsided. The hours ticked by. By dawn my hands were filthy and I had stopped feeling sorry for myself. I no longer wanted to die. I just wanted to go home.

I never saw the Siamese cat again. Three days later I was back with my New Zealand family. I have known many cats since then, but I will never forget the smelly stranger who eased the pain of my darkest night and propelled me toward the start of a happy and rewarding new life.

Jenny Lynch
Auckland
New Zealand

Write to me ...
Jenny Lynch
42A Sylvania Crescent
Lynfield, Auckland
NEW ZEALAND

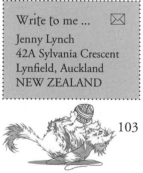

The dog who caught the bus

Many years ago a black Labrador cross caught a bus in the center of Truro, Cornwall, England. It was quite alone. The lady conductor tried to persuade the dog to get off but it sat, doggedly determined.

The dog alighted at the terminus on Trelander Estate, high above the city, where relatives lived with whom I used to spend holidays. It made its way to a house adjacent to the playing field. There it sat for some time, until the house owner gave it food and water and, failing to determine ownership, gave it a home.

There it lived happily for five years, until one day – some would have it that it was the same date (it was certainly close) – the dog retraced its steps to the bus stop, caught the bus down to the city center, debussed and disappeared into the crowds of shoppers, never to be seen again. Well, not by anyone in this story.

My uncle told me about it some 40 years ago. Conjecture had it that the dog may have belonged to someone who'd been imprisoned, and it somehow knew he'd been released. As we do not know the truth of the matter, it will remain a mystery. That is, unless there is a reader who knows differently.

Gerry S Rose
Newport
Wales

Compassion and grace

In our senior years, along with our two baby toy poodles, we moved to a retirement village which happily allows pets. They became the pride and joy of us and of our children. But back in the olden days there was also Abbey, a golden retriever, and her story should be told.

Abbey was the daughter of the great Kyvalley Kyva and Kyvalley Fairsky, both of whom appear in the history of the development of the breed in Australia. We acquired her at the age of 18 months from Bob Philp (a name the oldies will remember) when his council insisted he reduce the number of dogs he had in residence.

Abbey was an Australian champion and, as far as we know, the first show breeding golden retriever in the ACT. She produced champion children and grandchildren, but it was not her show career that marked her as unusual. It was her empathy with her master, my late husband, that made her a remarkable dog.

The two attended the Companion Dog School in Canberra, and Abbey was possibly the slowest working golden retriever ever known to the club. However, anyone who attended the classes, or saw the two working as a team, never failed to be impressed. You see, my husband was an incomplete quadriplegic as a result of a birth injury, and Abbey could adjust to his strange awkward gait, his stumbles and his falls.

At the time, Bruce was doing some research at the guide dog center in Melbourne, where he acquired a stiff-handled harness for 'his girl'. Abbey, in fact, became a mobile handrail that was strong and agile enough to adapt to any change in balance or a misplaced foot. With her he became more mobile, and together they ventured out into the bush and unfamiliar public buildings. She could take him up long flights of steps, like the old Parliament House, before the days when handrails were installed. She could take him through the bush, and up quite steep slopes as she clawed her way and hung onto small crevices, while he pulled himself up on her as though she were glued to the rock face.

As Bruce became more mobile and built up his exercise tolerance through her, he was able to go solo in the less threatening areas. But

Abbey forever kept a watchful eye out for any mishap and, should he fall, she was there before he hit the ground, sitting herself solidly in front of him, presenting herself as a solid pillar on which he could pull himself up.

Abbey's concern for disabled persons did not stop with her master. When a therapeutic playgroup for handicapped children was started in the ACT, Abbey joined the group. The children, who had previously been treated in the 'hospital environment', were delighted to come along to play with the doggy and receive a bit of physio while they were there.

For the children who cried when being rolled over the conventional roller equipment to relax their spasm, Abbey provided a nice padded shape for rolling, and what child could resist his or her turn to roll over this lovable soft toy? Weather permitting, she was even prepared to provide physio services outside under a tree, for children who were still timid of the hospital building.

Only once did she show any sign of disapproval. It was when one disturbed child deliberately ran over her tail with his wheelchair. She accepted this, such was her nature, but when my husband said, 'You were a naughty boy. You did that deliberately' one clear minute after the event, Abbey turned round and said *Grr* … the only cross utterance in her long life.

Clare Ford
Dandenong, Victoria
Australia

Write to me …
Clare Ford
c/- Smarter than Jack
PO Box 27003
Wellington
NEW ZEALAND

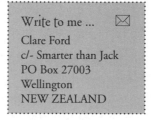

Charlie the movie critic

Back in the 1960s, I had a yellow-headed South American parrot. He was very smart and had been taught to do many clever things. He could bark like a small dog, cluck like a chicken, sing (although he was terribly off-key), and whistle better than any person I have ever heard. He also learned to repeat my husband's name and said *Hello* when the phone rang. If someone knocked on the door he would say *Come in* – and they did. They were certain a person had told them to enter.

But, for all his wisdom, he had never really replied directly to what was said to him, until one day when I had been watching a western movie on television. When it was over I turned off the TV, got up and said, 'Well, Charlie, how'd you like that cowboy show?'

Clear as you please, he replied, 'Pretty darn good.' I could hardly believe my ears. I thought, 'What a smart bird you are, Charlie.'

Rose-Ann Kirkeeng
Hudson's Hope, British Columbia
Canada

A doggy wake

When my mother was a teenager, she went to stay on a remote farm in the King Country with her Auntie Annie Grice. During the time she was there, word came through that a brother of her aunt's had died suddenly while at a stock sale.

Findlay McDougall had lived alone on another remote farm in the Upper Retaruke district. The undertakers took him to the mortuary and later to another town to be buried, so he never returned to his

farm. As he was a single man of 45 years, a neighbor looked after his stock until some decision could be made as to his estate.

About a week after his death my mother and her aunt traveled to his farm to deal with his clothes and the goods inside his house. My mother was asked to take her Uncle Findlay's clothes from the house and hang them on the clothes line to air. These were clothes that had been in the house all along.

Findlay's four dogs, which were having the freedom of a run loose from the chain at the time, immediately went and sat under the clothes hanging over the line and began to howl. My mother said the sound was so eerie and heart-wrenching that after an hour or two her Aunt Annie and she could stand it no longer and took the clothes back inside. Immediately, the dogs stopped their howling and went voluntarily back to their kennels.

How could those dogs have known their master was dead and given him the equivalent of a doggy send-off?

Celia Geary
Feilding
New Zealand

Write to me ...
Celia Geary
73 Denbigh Street
Feilding 5600
NEW ZEALAND

To dunk or not to dunk

Just a few days ago, my wife and I were having our lunch and looking out the window at the bright spring sunshine. After a long Thunder Bay winter, the warm sun was a welcome guest indeed. While we were peeking at the garden, we noticed a heavy Northern Ontario crow (not to be confused with the even heavier raven) pulling a piece of what looked like bread or bagel out of the neighbor's eaves trough. It was dripping wet and the crow proceeded to pull apart and devour the treat. Soon the crow had finished his meal and flew off to the north.

We laughed at the thought of our neighbor tossing bits of bread onto the roof to feed the birds – unusual, but not out of the question. As we started in on our tea and cookies, we noticed the crow return with a new hunk of bread … which he proceeded to dunk into the eaves trough for a good soaking. After a few moments, he pulled it out and finished his second course. He then had a few drinks of water, before flying off to the north again. The process was repeated several times.

Now we were amazed. This crow was finding tidbits of bread an unknown number of city blocks to the north and returning to this one plugged eaves trough to make his meal easier and more palatable.

Next time you're dunking a biscuit, donut or cookie, try to remember the crow and know that you're enjoying a true creature comfort!

Eric Adriaans
Thunder Bay, Ontario
Canada

Write to me …
email Eric
adriaans@tbaytel.net

He gave her his most treasured possession

Taj was an apricot spoodle – the intentional result of a cocker spaniel mum and poodle dad. He was asleep under his favorite chair one day, and I was sitting on the floor reading a letter that brought back sad memories. Silent tears were flowing.

Taj rushed over and frantically licked away my tears. This made me dissolve in great sobs. So my beloved Taj dashed from the room out into the garden, returning with his most treasured possession, a huge smelly old bone, stored away for a future banquet. He deposited it in my lap and then covered me in wet kisses!

Patsy Lambert
Auckland
New Zealand

Taj wanted to comfort Patsy

Was it a fox's funeral?

I'm incredibly fortunate to live in the woods, but living among nature can have its downside, especially when confronting such majestic beasts as mountain lions or bears.

I've had some close encounters with mountain lions, almost falling over a huge male as I walked backwards to warn some neighbors of his presence. I met another lion more recently and discovered much about nature, although I've been studying coyotes and other animals for many years. There's just so much we don't know.

I was driving up my road late one evening when I saw a large tan animal trotting toward my car. Thinking it was my neighbor's German shepherd Lolo, I stopped and opened my door to say hello, only to hear Lolo barking behind me. I was face to face with a male mountain lion. He stared at me, seemed to shrug his shoulders, and walked off. I slammed the car door shut and went home with all my senses on fire.

Next morning my neighbor said Lolo had found a fox carcass so I went to look at it. The fox, a formerly healthy male, had clearly been killed by the lion (I'll spare you the gory details) but his body was intact and partially covered with branches, dirt and some of the fox's own fur. It looked as if the lion had tried to cover his prey. I checked the carcass the next morning and it was still partially covered and unchanged from the day before.

Two days later I headed out at first light to hike with my companion, Jethro. I wanted no more surprises. I looked down the road and saw a small red female fox trying to cover the carcass. I was fascinated, for she was deliberately orienting her body so that when she kicked debris with her hind legs it would cover her friend, perhaps her mate. She'd kick dirt, stop, look at the carcass, and intentionally kick again. I observed this 'ritual' for a short while.

A few hours later, I saw that the carcass was now fully buried. I uncovered it and saw that it had been decapitated and partially eaten. No one to whom I have spoken – naturalists and professional biologists alike – has ever seen a red fox bury another red fox. I don't know if the female fox was intentionally trying to bury her friend, but there's no reason to assume that she wasn't. Perhaps she was grieving and I was observing a fox funeral.

I have no doubt that foxes and other animals have rich and deep emotional lives. Back in 1947 a naturalist on the East Coast saw a male fox lick his mate as she lay dead, and the male also protected his mate quite vigorously. Perhaps he too was showing respect for a dead friend.

I was lucky to have this series of encounters, for nature doesn't hold court at our convenience. Much happens in the complex lives of our animal kin to which we're not privy, but when we're fortunate to see animals at work, how splendid it is.

Marc Bekoff
Boulder, Colorado
United States

Marc Bekoff teaches courses in animal behavior at the University of Colorado in Boulder. He has published many books, including *Strolling with our Kin*, *The Smile of a Dolphin*, *Minding Animals*, *The Ten Trusts* (with Jane Goodall), *Encyclopedia of Animal Behavior*, and *Animal Passions and Beastly Virtues*.

Journey of an old warrior

When I was 14, my grandfather came to live with us, bringing his old dog, a Scotch terrier named Tess. They matched one another perfectly. Like him, she had a lot of white hair and not too many teeth, although the ones she did have were sharp and white. They went everywhere together and Tess slept every night at the end of my grandfather's bed, much to my mother's disgust.

Granddad had found Tess as a pup in an alley, foraging for food. She'd been abandoned, and was skin and bones and covered in fleas. My grandfather gathered her up in his great strong arms, wrapped her in his seaman's jacket and took her home. From that time on the two were inseparable.

My grandfather had his own boat, and sailed around the New Zealand coast delivering supplies to many of the small towns, which in those days had few means of communication with the outside world. He taught Tess tricks, which she would perform on request. She could count by barking up to five, and bounce a ball with her paw and catch it on her nose. This was always followed by her jumping into Granddad's arms and giving him a kiss.

Like my grandfather, she was an old warrior and as she got older her scars showed. One of her ears had a jagged edge where she'd been in a fight with a large tomcat, and her hind leg dragged as arthritis dug into the joint. Her eyesight was not as sharp as it had been and sometimes she banged into doors or tables, but her sense of smell was amazing, especially if there was food to be had.

One day she went missing. My grandfather put up a reward of £500, a huge amount in those days. I walked the streets with him every day after school, calling her name and asking people if they had seen her, but no one had. We put an advertisement in the newspaper and over the radio, but the telephone stayed silent and there was no sign that she still existed.

My grandfather was desolate. One day as I was passing his room, the door was open and I saw him holding up to his face the old blanket that she used to lie on. He was crying deep painful sobs, and

I crept away with a sense of sorrow and tragedy invading my soul that no amount of work or play could erase.

Two months went by and life went on. My father suggested that we get another dog but my grandfather refused the offer and went to lie on his bed, something he did more and more.

It was Sunday and we were sitting at the table eating our usual roast dinner when my mother, her fork suspended in the air, asked, 'What's that noise?' We listened and could hear a faint scratching, scuffling sound at the door. Then nothing.

My father and grandfather stood up. I can still see them. Two big men, looking at one another, the same thought flying through the air between them, and suddenly they were smiling. 'Tess!' they said together as they bolted for the door.

There she lay. How far she had walked we would never know. There were no pads left on her feet, and small bloody prints marked their way to our house. Around her neck was the chewed end of a thick rope that had tied her, and which she had bitten through to free herself and begin the long journey home. Vast amounts of fur were missing, and scabs and lice covered her skin. One eye was shut and she was panting in small painful gasps, but when my grandfather picked her up and held her to his chest she licked him and managed a soft bark.

We all cried, even my mother. My grandfather telephoned the vet and although it was Sunday he came to the house. 'She has walked a very, very long way to have her paws in such a condition,' he said. He was genuinely distressed to see the small dog in such a pitiful way. 'She must have great courage and suffered a great deal,' he added, and I saw tears waver down my grandfather's cheeks.

Tess was washed, bandaged, given an injection and later fed. All through that night and for the whole of the next week, my grandfather stayed by the side of the little dog, feeding, bathing and caring for her.

Tess recovered and lived to fight another day. She showed few side effects from her epic journey, but we noticed that neither she nor my grandfather ever let the other out of their sight again.

Ann French
Tauranga
New Zealand

Write to me ...
email Ann
bluedahlia123@gmail.com

A memorial?

This happened a couple of years ago. It moved me very much and I feel privileged to have witnessed it. My friend witnessed it as well.

While working in my paddock, I noticed that in an adjoining paddock, some distance away, there was a dead cow. About 15–20 other cows were forming a tight circle around the dead cow.

I stopped what I was doing and watched in amazement. The cows were keeping the young calves, who were obviously curious, from entering the circle by closing ranks and mooing at them to stay away.

Once the circle was tightly formed, with all the cattle facing inwards toward the dead one, the one and only bull moved to the dead cow. He looked, smelt it and circled around it before resuming his position in the circle. One by one, the cows then moved forward and did the same, each then resuming its position in the circle. This continued until all had done it. All the while they kept the calves away. This took about 50–60 minutes. They all then walked slowly away, at which time the calves had a quick look and a sniff and went away also.

It was as though the cattle were having their own memorial service and saying their good-byes. It was truly amazing.

Gai Hovey
Trentham, Victoria
Australia

Write to me ...
Gai Hovey
PO Box 73
Trentham VIC 3458
AUSTRALIA

Why doesn't Bruce enjoy his walks?

I have a two-year-old red-eared turtle, Bruce. He lives in a tank indoors. I feel concerned that he doesn't get to walk around enough so I like to take him outside to get some fresh air and exercise. However, whenever I do, he always heads straight for the nearest thing to hide under. How can I make him relax and enjoy this time in the fresh air and sunshine?

Can you offer any advice? Contact us at SMARTER than JACK.

9

Smart animals teach us lessons

A grateful dragonfly

Hummingbirds occasionally need rescuing when they fly into our garage in Shingletown, California and beat against the windows, unable to find their way back outside.

One day I heard the sound again and looked for a little bird. Instead it was a huge, shiny blue dragonfly. As I tried to open the window, in his fright over my hand being near he tangled himself in a large spider's web that had formed over the winter while we were snow birding in Arizona. Being unsure about his ability to bite or sting, I wrapped part of the web around a stick, pulled it loose with the beautiful bug inside and carried it out into the backyard.

I started to gently pull the web away from the dragonfly. As my hand came near he panicked again, beating his wings and struggling until he broke free. He was up in the air in a flash as I watched.

Suddenly, about ten feet or so up, he stopped, slowly turned himself around like a tiny helicopter and looked down at me for what seemed the longest time. I said, 'Good-bye! Be careful!' and he left. I tried to follow him with my eyes but he disappeared over the top of the garage.

Never again will a bug be just a bug to me. Who would think one would have the intelligence and emotion to feel grateful and say thank you.

Mary Ann Rais
Redding, California
United States

Write to me …
email Mary Ann
maryrais@yahoo.com

The smallest pet, for the smallest time

It was there as soon as I opened the door. Small, round, fluffy, helpless and just about to be trodden on. I picked it up and it still felt vulnerable, wings trembling in my fumbling human hands. Yet somehow, even in this flustered state, it was maintaining some sort of dignity. It didn't waste energy trying to avoid me. I thought of the other ones I'd found – some would recover from being stunned and live to fly away; others were frailer, perhaps more injured, and quietly died.

It's sad when that happens, because I've always loved bumblebees. This was my chance to save one. I got a little honey and put it on a tissue with the bumblebee. The creature crawled weakly toward the liquid on the tissue and dipped in a proboscis. The restoration of energy was the only hope – it's not as if you can give surgery to a bumblebee!

While the bee sucked, I carried it to the most fragrant bush in the garden and looked at all the creatures crawling, jumping and flying all over the yellow flowers. Red and orange spotted butterflies fluttered in hot summer air. Another bumblebee was doing its rounds of this fruitful bush. It seemed glowing with health, its coat shining in defined yellow and coal black.

Mine looked a little dusty in comparison. As if it had seen into my mind, it perked up a bit and began expertly cleaning its 'fur' of the tiny bits of debris. Six black limbs elegantly covered its entire body more efficiently than a back-scrubber, reminding me of a cat grooming itself.

After a good half hour of visibly depleting the blob of honey, the bumblebee became more active, walking all over my hands and flexing its wings. All of a sudden it lifted off and flew up, spiraling dizzily toward the top of the willow tree, until it was lost in blue sky. My new pet – gone.

We think we're so clever – and, to a certain extent, we are – but, for all the millennia we've been on this earth, will we ever be able to fly like that, unaided, many times our own height, and from the brink of death? With only its tiny body, the bumblebee accomplished more than Daedalus or any amount of modern aerodynamic study could possibly achieve. To fly self-sufficiently – how naturally clever.

Pippa Jane Ström
Foxton
New Zealand

Write to me ...
email Pippa
pipskiromanov@gmail.com

Barney, dear rat

My grandmother and I were out for a stroll in a forested park. We were talking about Freddy, the hooded rat I'd had as a child, for I'd recently decided I wanted another pet rat.

I was looking up at the trees, when my grandmother (whom I call Mom) stopped and said, 'Will you look here!' At her feet was a tiny white rat. A *pet* rat.

'Mom, he wants our help.' It was Sunday afternoon and there were many people and dogs out walking. How did he know to pick us? Mom bent down to pick him up, but a dog also saw him and barked, which scared the young rat back into the woods.

'We have to take him home, Mom. This is too uncanny.'

Just as flabbergasted, she said, 'Yes, but I doubt you'll find him now.'

'We have to. He'll die out here, he'll get eaten by a hawk or coyotes. He knows he doesn't belong here – why else did he come up to you?'

Mom and I made a note of landmarks so that my sweetheart Christopher and I could return with a live squirrel trap and a hunk of cheese. To avoid onlookers we went after dark. We found the area by the trail and shone our flashlights on ferns, moss and fallen branches – but no white rat.

'He's probably on the other side of the park by now,' Christopher said glumly.

'No, he's here, I *feel* it.' I didn't care if I sounded foolish; I somehow knew he was nearby and in desperate need. Just then we saw a flash of white fur. With renewed enthusiasm – and stealth – Christopher placed the trap on the ground and approached a hollow log, and there he was. Christopher held out some cheese. I expected the rat to grab it, but he took it ever so slowly, placed it deeper into his hidey-hole and came back to stare at us.

This blinking contest went on for about half an hour. Just as we were ready to call it quits and try again the next day, he walked slowly into the trap. He ignored the cheese, as though he was thinking, *I'm tired, let's just get out of here*.

At home, we found he had gray patches over his eyes and ears, forming a diamond-shaped white patch on his forehead. I saw a TV documentary that said horses and other animals are bred for this

Barney became a treasured family pet

'white diamond' as they're often more docile. I was curious to find out.

We named him Barney because we'd found him in Burnaby. I shampooed him and noticed he had some bloody wounds around his neck, so I held him firmly while Christopher plucked the ticks out with tweezers. Our new friend squealed blue murder. I lost my grip for a second and he chomped down on my thumb. Now we were both squealing and bleeding all over the sink. I left to get a tetanus shot and painkillers. I forgave him and felt confident he'd eventually come around.

For the first week, Barney was so scared he'd try to hide his head. When we called to him he'd freeze on the spot – we joked that he was testing the Ninja Secret of Invisibility. Slowly, he let us handle him. We cured him of nipping by shouting 'No!' and putting him back in his cage each time, and we toilet-trained him the same way.

Before long, he would stand at his cage door, eagerly waiting to be picked up. We'd let him roam around the couch, and used affection instead of food to get him to come when he was called. Eventually, we let him scamper around the living room because we knew he wouldn't hide anymore. Friends were amazed when they saw a rat sitting on his bum or lying on his back being tickled under the chin and making a funny noise which we now know is rat laughter.

One night, I was ill but pulled myself out of bed as I knew Barney would be waiting for me. When I took him out, he started licking my hand the way a dog does when it's grateful. Barney had never done this before. He looked up at me, then climbed onto my shoulder to lick my ear where the infection was. It was as though he knew where it hurt and wanted to fix it for me.

He has become a true family pet, cheering our lives with his antics and affection. He has evolved from a frightened throwaway to a rag doll on our laps. At the time he appeared, I was going through some traumatizing problems. It was through Barney that my belief in divine intervention was rekindled. He reminds me that if I keep my survival instinct up when life looks bleak and persevere in harsh conditions, if I ask for help when I'm lost and take risks when I'm scared, there will come surprising rewards. Most of all, he helped me to regain my belief in happy endings.

Sheila Morrison
Gabriola Island, British Columbia
Canada

Write to me ...
Sheila Morrison
986 Lewis Close
Gabriola Island BC V0R 1X2
CANADA
or email
smorrisonhamilton@yahoo.ca

Don't tell me they are silly galahs!

It had been very hot that year in Whyalla and I heard his complaints coming down to me along the back lane as I worked in the garden. Eventually, they disturbed me enough to go and see what was causing the cacophony.

There the poor fellow was, in a tin cage up against a corrugated fence, experiencing the force of that summer's heat. I went and knocked on the door, and was soon faced by this male character with a glass of beer and a cigarette in one hand, holding the screen door open with the other. I advised him of the condition of the galah in the cage and told him I would help him move it into the shade.

He said, 'If he troubles you that much, you can have him; I'm sick and tired of his noise.'

'Okay,' I said, 'Does that include the cage?'

'All right,' was the reply as the door slammed shut.

So that was how I got a galah in a cage, when I can't stand seeing birds in cages.

About two weeks after this, while hanging out washing, this point came home to me as Cockey and I eyed each other. He wasn't really happy, that was plain to see. So I opened the cage door and said, 'Come and help me to hang the washing out.' Bit by bit he came out, and from then on he'd fly onto the hoist with a lot of squawking.

I continued to chatter away to him while hanging out the clothes, and gradually he quietened down. Eventually putting my hand up for him to hop onto, he did and I put him back into the cage.

Each day from then on, while I was in the backyard Cockey was given the freedom of the yard.

People told me I had to clip his wing or he would fly away and, if that happened, the other birds could kill him as he didn't know his place in the scheme of things. But his wings weren't clipped and he didn't fly away, except to follow me in the car when I went to see

my sister and wait for me while perched on her next-door neighbor's TV aerial.

When the time came for me to go home he'd fly just above the car, and when we got home he'd hop into his cage and wait for me to shut him in. This was always done to keep him safe from cats. Cockey was a much happier bird!

One day I heard quite a cacophony in the backyard and, looking out, the galahs had all landed on the lawn and were chattering away merrily to each other; and there was Cockey, who was nearly beside himself with excitement. I figured they had come to pick him up, and so the next day I made sure the cage door was open in case they dropped in again. They did, and they *had* come to collect Cockey, for when they flew off, he went with them.

Well, I felt quite selfish for a few minutes and wished I had clipped his wing, but pretty soon that rubbish was put to one side and I got on with the day.

We were sitting down for tea when Cockey's squawk came from the back door, and there he was, saying 'hello' – before he hopped into the cage for the night. He chattered away to me for quite a while, telling me of his exciting day as I locked his door to keep him safe. Then, putting his head down into his wing, he went to sleep.

The next day, the galah buddies turned up and off went Cockey with them. For two or maybe three weeks this went on, until one night Cockey didn't come home. He'd got his sea legs at last on the big ocean of life.

I thought that was the end of the story, but to this day – many years later – I still can't be sure!

At last, after years of bringing up three children on my own, I found myself at home alone. It was a pretty awesome experience.

There'd been no time to really experience my own company and frankly I wasn't used to it.

There wasn't the money to buy a car, so I bought a motorbike and was going to tour Eyre's Peninsula on it. Well, the first day, I set off on a small trip to test myself out. Iron Knob looked like a 'fair go' for a first trip, and before long there I was in Iron Knob.

Getting braver by the minute and still with plenty of daylight, my sights got set on Kimba. Probably about a quarter of the way there, I was suddenly hit with the immense loneliness of Australia, and as that thought came home to me, I began to panic. I mean, I really panicked! In fact, I was so scared that my teeth began to chatter and my breathing became shallower and shallower, and my steering of the bike wasn't straight. However, along that long, long flat road there wasn't a car, a house, not even a sheep in the paddock. I was beginning to think I wasn't ready for this.

With a streak of stubbornness that I hadn't been aware of until then, I kept going, knowing that the road wouldn't be tackled again if I gave up.

Then, out of the blue, they came and surrounded me. There must have been at least 30 – if not more – and the racket they made as they squawked and called to each other could be heard over the roar of the bike. They spread out on either side of me and some flew along just in front of me; some were so close to me that I could have reached out and touched them.

I was sure it would be just a momentary interlude that at least broke my panic and gave me back to myself, but it wasn't … they stayed with me, mile after mile after mile. They chattered and chortled, swooped and dipped, and managed to fill me with their wonderful free joy of life. Those galahs put new life into me and opened the doors of freedom for me … and suddenly I thought

of Cockey … I remembered how he had followed me in the car and how I had slowly opened the doors of freedom for him … was it possible? Could he be the initiator of this flock and their wonderful and strange behavior? I yelled aloud his name, but they all just squawked back at me and continued with me along that long, long road – when, quite suddenly, they weaved off to the left and disappeared into the bush as I topped the hill and there lay the little town of Kimba in the next valley.

Stopping the bike, I just sat there, marveling at what had to be a truly rare and wonderful experience. Had Cockey really been among them, or was some group consciousness just keeping me company because they had heard how I had helped a buddy? I remember how my mother used to say when something unexplained happened to her, 'God works in strange and mysterious ways His wonders to perform.'

Well, all that was a few years back. I'm 72 years old now, but the wonder of that experience makes me realize how little we humans really know about our fellow creatures on this earth, never mind on Mars.

Ruth Lee-Bowie
Whyalla
South Australia

They had to say good-bye

Madison was a bull mastiff who loved her humans unconditionally, especially her boy Mikey.

Anyone who has shared a home with a bull mastiff knows that if their dinner bowl is still full then something is wrong. A call to the vet suggested we bring her in for an examination.

She had congestive heart failure, although she was still young. The cardiologist confirmed that nothing could be done. The next morning came and it was evident what I had to do. I thought it would be best for my son to think she'd passed peacefully during the night. I would tell him this when he came home from school. I gave her a big hug and a kiss, and told her I loved her and this was the best thing for her.

We got out of the car but she refused to move. I think she knew she hadn't said all her good-byes. As I coaxed her into the clinic it was evident that she needed to see her boy one last time. I canceled the appointment and said I would reschedule for the following day. I brought her home for one last night.

Madison got to spend her last night on the floor with my son, and the next morning she headed for the door as if to say, *I'm ready now.*

Madison wanted to say goodbye to Mikey

Although this was the saddest and hardest thing to do, she taught me to communicate more with my son and let him share in making decisions.

Liz Senter
Prince Edward Island
Canada

Logan the afterthought

Logan nonchalantly eyed the addition in the window over the couch. While others scrambled to escape the icy blast and stern hum of the air conditioner, he sauntered purposely toward it. Seated on the back of the couch he carefully scrutinized every inch. Then he delicately explored all the nooks and crannies with his paw, while turning his head from side to side and up and down. He discerned that you can loosen the front filter panel with a gentle tug, or slide open the control door behind which buttons huddle waiting to be pushed. Logan has been lobbying to study engineering at MIT since we brought him home.

Previously named Partner, he had been the singleton afterthought selected to keep the lonely Tiki company in her cage at the shelter as she recovered from being dumped on the parkway at 60 miles an hour. He had hardly been noticed before and no one knew his history.

At home, it immediately became apparent that Tiki would have been happier without a partner – especially this one – and Logan's calm shelter demeanor had been a front for the tiger that lurked in his heart. Equally at home dumping the trash on the floor or standing on the toaster, it took him all of a week to learn how to open doors – both lever and round.

At first, he was really into garbology. Barrels of booty had to be minutely examined, followed by rooting through the recycles to study how things rolled and clanked on the tiles. How easy to delight his eager audience, with papers flying and cans colliding. His electrical engineering career started some time after we relocated the trash can inside the cabinet under the sink. Not wanting him to be toast or lost, we unplugged all the appliances and locked all the doors.

Even though engineers are not known for their intuitive nature, Logan fine-tuned that aspect of his psyche. He can divine precisely those things you don't want him to do, and do them with flair. He intuits when you're about to open a door for him to squeeze outside or a closet to get into to search for hidden garbage or electrical equipment.

Logan may not have a degree in electronics yet, but he does have a PhD in 'the moves'. If you are not sufficiently obsequious, he will fix his green-eyed gaze on you and strut his golden stuff as he choreographs the John Wayne glide toward you, punctuated with a full stretch – one paw pointed directly at you, his victim.

Now, you might think life has been easy and charmed for Logan. Not so. Challenged for nine months by a respiratory infection brought on by a rabies vaccination, he had to be medicated several times a day with up to four meds at a time. He also had to sit in a steamy shower morning and evening to sneeze out the infection that was killing him. He always slept with me so that he could be rushed into the shower if he needed it. And many nights he did. Then there is the cardiomyopathy. But a regimen created for him by an holistic vet finds him a lovable rascal still.

Logan has accepted everything with good humor. Even on his sickest day he had time to play with a feather, get into trouble, be mischievous – but, most of all, be loving. He would tear around the house nipping at everyone's shanks, empty the trash on the floor

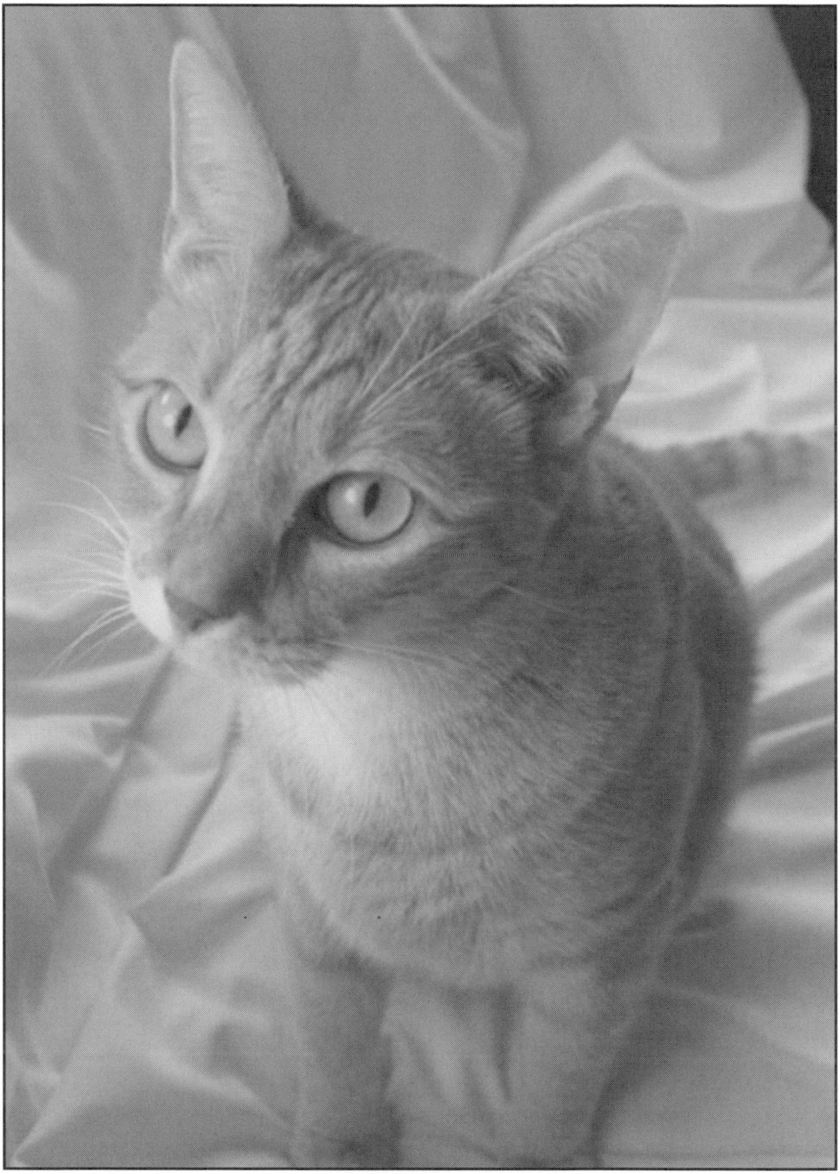

'In a room full of hearts, Logan is the soul'

and then claw right up your clothes for a snuggle or flop down for a snooze, flinging his arm around the chosen of the moment. He's the first at the door to greet and the last to say good-bye. He turns his blessed sunny face up for a kiss and a nuzzle, before deigning to sit in your lap or lie by your side, waiting to have sung 'Oh, my love, my Logan'. In a room full of hearts, Logan is the soul.

This kaleidoscope of lessons – Logan – searched for or created joy on even his sickest days. He loves everyone and believes everyone loves him. He's never taken umbrage that he wasn't even noticed, except as a companion for Tiki, and ignominiously named Partner. He's never been offended that no one had noted his jade green eyes or golden hair. This self-assured and self-actualized golden boy doesn't need anyone's good opinion, but he graciously accepts it.

Despite URI, cardiomyopathy and electrical explorations, Logan has been both prince and elder democratic statesman for four years and shows no sign of vacating the positions. Well, prince or not, his bid to study at MIT will go unfulfilled. He'll have to attend during one of his other nine lives. For now he'll study at home, where his joyful presence is needed. I'll get him some appliances at yard sales this week, though.

Afterthought, indeed!

Madelyn Filipski
Cape May County, New Jersey
United States

These crows knew how to crack nuts

It was a lovely September afternoon and I should have been working. But as I sat in my home office looking out the window, I longed to be outside in the fresh air.

My quiet residential street boasts a number of leafy walnut trees, and it's entertaining to watch the antics of the birds and squirrels who make their homes in them. So it wasn't really my fault that I couldn't concentrate; the activities outside my window were just too entertaining. In fact, I'd have to blame it on a couple of crows.

Now, crows have never been my favorite birds. I've always seen them as a bit of a nuisance, pulling garbage out of bins and waking me in the early morning with their squawks. But these two ingenious birds made me see crows in a different light.

As I watched, they scooped up walnuts from under the trees and flew with them to the telephone wires above the tarmac. I was amazed they could even hold the large nuts in their beaks, let alone fly with them. And I was fascinated to see the crows drop the walnuts onto the road, swoop down to pick them up and fly back to their perch on the wires.

They would then drop the nuts a second time on the hard surface. Unbelievably, they were using the principles of physics to crack the nuts. Occasionally a car would drive by, and I noticed that the crows would pick up their treasure and move swiftly to the roadside, hopping impatiently from foot to foot until the vehicle passed.

After the third or fourth drop the birds would land on the road, hold the walnut with one clawed foot and pry open the shell with their strong beaks. Finally, they'd pick out the sweet morsels and flap about, looking very proud of themselves. This process continued until the crows presumably had had their fill.

If I hadn't seen this extraordinary evidence of their intelligence, I don't think I'd have believed it. With a chuckle and a new appreciation of the engineering genius of crows, I decided to follow their industrious example and get back to work.

Donna Deacon
Langley, British Columbia
Canada

Too many birds spoil the flavor

Being a couple of city workers, our ideal getaway place was a deserted beach. We found one north of Colville on the Coromandel Peninsula. Far from the crowds, we set the billy to boil and lay back in the shade on a crimson blanket of pohutukawa flowers.

No cars, no cellphones, no other beings … wait, there was one: a quietly watchful red-billed gull.

We tossed him a crust of bread. The gull snatched it up, turned and scurried down the shell-bank. He then sauntered across 15 meters of sand, dropped the crust in the tide and waited for the next incoming wave. It returned his bread, salted and moistened, to his feet. Having savored the morsel the bird strutted back up the beach, over the shells, and stoically stared at us.

A solitary seagull is a fascination to those of us used to flocks of skirling gulls squabbling over litter in city playgrounds. So we offered the lone gull another crust, which he again took the time to carry down to the tide for seasoning.

When he next came up the beach, a companion gull flew in. We threw them each some bread and they toddled off together to process it in the sea before eating.

Only one more bird joined us for lunch, but when it did there was an immediate change in behavior. The new imperative was to gulp down on the spot whatever was for the taking. Salt and water with your bread? Not likely. Their preference for a little relish with their food was quickly forgotten in the company of competitors.

That day, three gulls on the Coromandel coast presented a charming illustration of how one is opportunity, two is company, three is a crowd – and crowds definitely spoil the quality of life.

Christine Mackinder
Waitakere City
New Zealand

Stewart the joyful

Stewart was a small bouvier puppy, one of 11. We noticed that he got the least of the nursing and the most knocking about by his siblings.

We counteracted that with extra bottle-feedings and by monitoring him in the whelping box, tucking him as often as we could under the protection of his mother's chin. But at about ten days we noticed that his front legs were always straight back and he was unable to knead his mother's teat for milk. The other puppies were starting to wobble about but he just lay there, whimpering plaintively.

The vet diagnosed fading puppy syndrome. He advised putting the pup aside in a box and making him comfortable with a hot-water bottle, a soft blanket and a stuffed bear, and he would just slip away.

Well, Stewart didn't think so. My husband was sleeping on a palette in the whelping room, to be near if any problems arose during the night. Stewart cried and fussed for quite a while. My husband felt that, dying or not, he must be missing the closeness of his mother and siblings. He tucked the pup into bed with him. Stewart settled down and they slept through the night together.

The next morning we put Stewart back in the whelping box and thought we would just let be what would be. We would bottle-feed him, make sure he didn't get too roughed up and let nature take its course.

Stewart rallied. It's true that he got knocked over a lot, and was constantly tromped on and squashed and pinned in uncomfortable places. When the pups were big enough to romp around outside, they would all pile out the door, trampling Stewart flat in the process. As they cavorted and ran about, Stewart was left behind by faster siblings, knocked over or stepped on. He reminded us of a tall, spindly-legged, top-heavy Louis IVth table. He was so stiff-legged that it took just a small shove to tip him over. But, every time, he got up and continued on.

The vet eventually diagnosed cellabellar hypoplasia, a congenital condition where the brain/nerve connection has not totally formed. The brain either forgets to send a message to the legs (for example, *Here is a sidewalk, lift your feet*) and other extremities or sends them the wrong messages.

Stewart drags his toes when he walks. It was two years before he wagged his stumpy little tail. Before that, he didn't know there was an appendage to wag. He falls down a lot. He trips over shadows across the path. He sometimes forgets halfway up a flight of stairs how to 'do' stairs, and stumbles. On the way down, he slides the last four or five steps.

Every time he falls down, not a whimper, not a yelp – he picks himself up, shakes the dirt and leaves from his beard, and shuffles on. He has a constant slap-silly smile on his face.

Whenever we feel put upon by the world, we watch Stewart. His positive attitude puts our self-pity to shame. Whenever we feel like quitting on something, we watch him. He picks himself up … and goes on. Whenever we feel short-changed, we watch Stewart and his quiet pleasure in a face rub with his favorite humans.

And Stewart teaches joy. We take him to a nearby field and let him run off-leash. He has the most awkward way of running I've ever seen. He exhausts himself 'running' in this peculiar fashion. But the joy! My husband and I stand at opposite ends of the field and Stewart runs back and forth between us. His front legs fly out to each side and windmill crazily to gain speed, while his back legs rabbit hop and sometimes get ahead of him. But the teddy bear eyes are bright and gleeful. He takes such grand, uninhibited joy in being able to run. Such joy with life, such joy with himself.

Other breeders have told us we should have put Stewart down. Ah no, our lives and the world would be so much smaller without him. Stewart's registered name is long and complicated; though a knightly name. But Stewart is a simple little guy with simple little pleasures; he's just Stewart the Joyful.

Linda Hegland
Port Coquitlam, British Columbia
Canada

Write to me …
Linda Hegland
1642 Robertson Avenue
Port Coquitlam BC V3B 1E1
CANADA

The naturalist

Wee Geordie is a brown and white stud llama whose intelligence has always amazed us.

Geordie is descended from a strain of Peruvian llamas called Ships of the Andes. Once used for transporting trade goods over the mountains, they are now bred and trained for recreational packing in the backcountry of British Columbia.

After all his ladies have been attended to in spring, Geordie lives in a paddock by himself. Being a boisterous, exuberant and social fellow, he sometimes gets lonely and much enjoys visitors.

One warm spring day, my daughter dropped off my two grandbabies for the day. Heather (three) and Brandon (five) love to come to Grandma and Grandpa's farm to visit and play with the llamas.

Geordie seems to enjoy small children, so I decide to take Brandon and Heather for a stroll through his paddock. With their pockets full of llama treats, off we go, Geordie following close behind, ever so gently taking offerings of llama cookies from sticky wee fingers. I keep the grandbabies close beside me for safety, for, although Geordie has always been gentle with them, it is in the back of my mind that we are on his turf, and stud llamas can be territorial.

Brandon exclaims over an unusually shaped stone. He picks it up for me to admire, then drops it in his pocket. Heather picks a pretty blue wildflower for Grandma's hair. Geordie seems as delighted as I am with the children's discoveries, reaching over their shoulders to look at each new treasure. A butterfly is next, bringing giggles of delight from Heather. A piece of old tree root shaped like a bird in flight is Brandon's find, and again Geordie sniffs it in apparent approval.

I'm enjoying myself immensely. My two precious grandbabies will soon be grown and gone. Today they are filled with wonder

at the marvels of the natural world around us and I wish I could prolong this time with them. Geordie senses my mood and rubs my shoulder with his nose in seeming accord. Then he wanders off to nibble tender new leaves from a nearby willow.

We continue on and Heather finds a ladybug. I tell her ladybugs are good for the garden because they eat the bugs that eat my plants. She considers this for a moment, then solemnly announces she will take the ladybug back to put in my garden.

Geordie is back, nudging Brandon and Heather as if rounding them up. Does he want us to leave? Had enough of people invading his territory? I caution him to be gentle, and he walks back to the willow, watching us. Something is going on here and I study him closely, puzzling over his odd behavior. Again he comes to nudge the children, and looks over at the willow. I have a sudden insight: this llama has been participating in the nature studies all along and has his own discovery to contribute. Then I chide myself for being silly. This is, after all, only an animal.

Geordie runs back to the willow and points with his nose at a fork in the tree part-way up, then looks over at us. By now I am sure he is trying to show us something. Taking both children by the hand, I walk over to the willow to investigate. I look where Geordie is pointing, brush the leaves aside, and here is the llama's discovery – a robin's nest! The nest is at eye level, and both children are clamoring to be lifted up. Brandon first, and as I lift him for a look the nest erupts with excited cheeping and four hungry mouths reach up to be fed. Brandon is enthralled, turns in my arms with glowing face to hug me and exclaims. 'Oh, Grandma, this is the *best* day!'

Heather's turn next … then I explain we'd better leave the nest so momma robin can feed her hungry youngsters. I turn to Geordie, feeling rather humbled. We humans always assume our superiority, when we would do well to pay closer attention to our four-legged companions. Geordie gives me a pleased look and seems to understand my appreciation. I rub his neck in thanks.

When Geordie turns his long graceful neck to acknowledge my thanks, his upper lip lifts and curls in an expression that is very much like a knowing grin. Then he escorts us back to the pasture gate. Time to go, for Grandpa has lunch waiting.

Bev Henry
Barriere, British Columbia
Canada

Wee Geordie gave his family a nature study lesson

Why do ducks need to cross the road?

My mother used to live in a unit, one of five grouped around a courtyard. In front of the units was a busy road, and at the back a quiet park with a creek.

Every year mother ducks would bring their chattering broods of ducklings to visit and the residents would feed them. It was safe there, with no dogs or cats to harm the families. Did they stick to the security of the park and the courtyard? They did not! Several times a day the mother ducks would be seen crossing the road followed by their hapless strings of ducklings, and when they returned there were often one or two babies missing. Where I live there are paddocks on my side of the road, with plentiful worms and water – everything a duck's heart could desire. But the ducks that try to raise families here insist on leading their babies to and fro across the road. Those that make it across (and we often find the sad, flattened remains of the ones who don't) have to contend with a resident hawk. Each mother hatches a dozen or so ducklings but is lucky if three or four survive.

Can you offer any advice? Contact us at SMARTER than JACK.

Why do sheep leap?

When a flock of sheep pass through a gateway most of them walk or canter, but a few leap in the air as if jumping over a fence – yet there is nothing there to jump over.

Can you offer any advice? Contact us at SMARTER than JACK.

The SMARTER than JACK story

We hope you've enjoyed this book. The SMARTER than JACK books are exciting and entertaining to create and so far we've raised over NZ$280,000 to help animals. We are thrilled!

Here's my story about how the SMARTER than JACK series came about.

Until late 1999 my life was a seemingly endless search for the elusive 'fulfilment'. I had this feeling that I was put on this earth to make a difference, but I had no idea how. Coupled with this, I had low self-confidence – not a good combination! This all left me feeling rather frustrated, lonely and unhappy with life. I'd always had a creative streak and loved animals. In my early years I spent many hours designing things such as horse saddles, covers and cat and dog beds. I even did a stint as a professional pet photographer.

Then I remembered something I was once told: do something for the right reasons and good things will come. So that's what I did. I set about starting Avocado Press and creating the first New Zealand edition in the SMARTER than JACK series. It was released in 2002 and all the profit went to the Royal New Zealand SPCA.

Good things did come. People were thrilled to be a part of the book and many were first-time writers. Readers were enthralled and many were delighted to receive the book as a gift from friends and family. The Royal New Zealand SPCA was over $43,000 better off and I received many encouraging letters and emails from readers and contributors. What could be better than that?

How could I stop there! It was as if I had created a living thing with the SMARTER than JACK series; it seemed to have a life all of its own. I now had the responsibility of evolving it. It had to continue to benefit animals and people by providing entertainment, warmth and something that people could feel part of. What an awesome responsibility and opportunity, albeit a bit of a scary one!

It is my vision to make SMARTER than JACK synonymous with smart animals, and a household name all over the world. The concept is already becoming well known as a unique and effective way for animal welfare charities to raise money, to encourage additional donors and to instil a greater respect for animals. The series is now in Australia, New Zealand, the United States, Canada and the United Kingdom.

Avocado Press, as you may have guessed, is a little different. We are about more than just creating books; we're about sharing information and experiences, and developing things in innovative ways. Ideas are most welcome too.

We feel it's possible to run a successful business that is both profitable and that contributes to animal welfare in a significant way. We want people to enjoy and talk about our books; that way, ideas are shared and the better it becomes for everyone.

Thank you for reading my story.

Jenny Campbell
Creator of SMARTER than JACK

Submit a story for our books

We are always creating more exciting books in the SMARTER than JACK series. Your true stories are continually being sought.

You can have a look at our website www.smarterthanjack.com. Here you can read stories, find information on how to submit stories, and read entertaining and interesting animal news. You can also sign up to receive the Story of the Week by email. We'd love to hear your ideas, too, on how to make the next books even better.

Guidelines for stories

- The story must be true and about a smart animal or animals.
- The story should be about 100 to 1000 words in length. We may edit it and you will be sent a copy to approve prior to publication.
- The story must be written from your point of view, not the animal's.
- Photographs and illustrations are welcome if they enhance the story, and if used will most likely appear in black and white.
- Submissions can be sent by post to SMARTER than JACK (see addresses on the following page) or via the website at www.smarterthanjack.com
- Include your name, postal and email address, and phone number, and indicate if you do not wish your name to be included with your story.
- Handwritten submissions are perfectly acceptable, but if you can type them, so much the better.
- Posted submissions will not be returned unless a stamped self-addressed envelope is provided.
- The writers of stories selected for publication will be notified prior to publication.
- Stories are welcome from everybody, and given the charitable nature of our projects there will be no prize money awarded, just recognition for successful submissions.

- Particpating animal welfare charities and Avocado Press have the right to publish extracts from the stories received without restriction of location or publication, provided the publication of those extracts helps promote the SMARTER than JACK series.

Where to send your story

Online

- Use the submission form at www.smarterthanjack.com or email it to submissions@smarterthanjack.com.

By post

- **In Australia**
  PO Box 170, Ferntree Gully, VIC 3156, Australia
- **In Canada and the United States**
  PO Box 819, Tottenham, ON, L0G 1W0, Canada
- **In New Zealand and rest of world**
  PO Box 27003, Wellington, New Zealand

Receive a free SMARTER than JACK gift pack

Did you know that around half our customers buy the SMARTER than JACK books as gifts? We appreciate this and would like to thank and reward those who do so. If you buy eight books in the SMARTER than JACK series we will send you a free gift pack.

All you need to do is buy your eight books and either attach the receipt for each book or, if you ordered by mail, just write the date that you placed the order in one of the spaces on the next page. Then complete your details on the form, cut out the page and post it to us. We will then send you your SMARTER than JACK gift pack. Feel free to photocopy this form – that will save cutting a page out of the book.

Do you have a dog or a cat? You can choose from either a cat or dog gift pack. Just indicate your preference.

Note that the contents of the SMARTER than JACK gift pack will vary from country to country, but may include:

- The SMARTER than JACK mini Collector Series
- SMARTER than JACK postcards
- Soft animal toy
- Books in the SMARTER than JACK series

Show your purchases here:

Book 1	Book 2	Book 3	Book 4
Receipt attached ☐ *or* Date ordered ________	Receipt attached ☐ *or* Date ordered ________	Receipt attached ☐ *or* Date ordered ________	Receipt attached ☐ *or* Date ordered ________
Book 5	**Book 6**	**Book 7**	**Book 8**
Receipt attached ☐ *or* Date ordered ________	Receipt attached ☐ *or* Date ordered ________	Receipt attached ☐ *or* Date ordered ________	Receipt attached ☐ *or* Date ordered ________

Complete your details:

Your name: ______________________________

Street address: ______________________________

City/town: ______________________________

State: ______________________________

Postcode: ______________________________

Country: ______________________________

Phone: ______________________________

Email: ______________________________

Would you like a cat or dog gift pack? CAT/DOG

Post the completed page to us:

- **In Australia**
  PO Box 170, Ferntree Gully, VIC 3156, Australia
- **In Canada and the United States**
  PO Box 819, Tottenham, ON, L0G 1W0, Canada
- **In New Zealand and rest of world**
  PO Box 27003, Wellington, New Zealand

Please allow four weeks for delivery.

Get more wonderful stories

Now you can receive a fantastic new-release SMARTER than JACK book every three months. That's a new book every March, June, September and December. The books are delivered to your door. It's easy!

Here's a sample of what you'd get if you signed up for four books over one year (option 2 on the order form) in September 2005:

- *Cats are SMARTER than JACK* in September 2005
- *Dogs are SMARTER than JACK* in December 2005
- *Heroic animals are SMARTER than JACK* in March 2006
- *Cheeky animals are SMARTER than JACK* in June 2006

Every time you get a book you will also receive a copy of *Smart Animals*, our members-only newsletter. Postage is included in the subscription price if the delivery address is in the United States, Canada, the United Kingdom, Australia or New Zealand.

You can also purchase existing titles in the SMARTER than JACK series. To purchase a book you can either go to your local bookstore or participating animal welfare charity, or order using the form at the end of the book.

How your purchase will help animals

The amount our partner animal welfare charities receive varies according to how the books are sold and the country in which they are sold. Contact your local participating animal welfare charity for more information.

In Australia

Smarter than Jack Limited is accepting orders on behalf of the RSPCA in Australia. Please send your order to:

SMARTER than JACK, PO Box 170, Ferntree Gully, VIC 3156

In Canada

The Canadian Federation of Humane Societies is accepting orders on behalf of the participating animal welfare charities in Canada, as listed below. Please send your order to:

CFHS, 102-30 Concourse Gate, Ottawa, ON, K2E 7V7

Please nominate from the following list the participating animal welfare charity that you would like to benefit from your book purchase:

- Alberta SPCA
- Bide A While Animal Shelter Society
- Calgary Humane Society
- Cochrane Humane Society
- Hamilton/Burlington SPCA
- Lakeland Humane Society
- Mae Bachur Animal Shelter
- Meadowlake and District Humane Society
- Newfoundland & Labrador SPCA
- Nova Scotia Humane Society
- Ontario SPCA
- Ottawa Humane Society
- PEI Humane Society
- Red Deer and District SPCA
- Saskatchewan SPCA
- SPA de l'Estrie
- Winnipeg Humane Society

In New Zealand

Please send your order to:

Royal New Zealand SPCA National Office, PO Box 15349, New Lynn, Auckland 1232

In the United Kingdom

Smarter than Jack Limited is accepting orders on behalf of the participating animal welfare charities in the United Kingdom, as listed below. Please send your order to:

SMARTER than JACK, FREEPOST NAT 11465, Northampton, NN3 6BR

Please nominate from the following list the participating animal welfare charity that you would like to benefit from your book purchase:

- Cats Protection
- Dogs Trust

In the United States

Smarter than Jack Limited is accepting orders on behalf of the participating animal welfare charities in the United States, as listed below. Please send your order to:

SMARTER than JACK, 45 High Street N, Thunder Bay, ON, P7A 5R1, CANADA

Please nominate from the following list the participating animal welfare charity that you would like to benefit from your book purchase:

- Alley Cat Allies
- American Humane Association
- Animal Rescue Foundation Inc.
- Cat Care Society
- Feral Friends Animal Rescue and Assistance
- Humane Society of Lewisville
- Jeff Davis County Humane Society
- People for the Ethical Treatment of Animals (PETA)
- Pets911
- West Plains Regional Animal Shelter

Rest of world

Please send your order to:

SMARTER than JACK, PO Box 27003, Wellington,
NEW ZEALAND

Purchase from your local bookstore

Your local bookstore should have the editions you want or, if not, be able to order them for you. If they can't get the books, the publisher Avocado Press can be contacted direct:

By email: orders@smarterthanjack.com
By post: Avocado Press Limited, PO Box 27003, Wellington,
NEW ZEALAND

Order online

To order online go to www.supportanimals.com

How much are the books?

- Australia $19.95
- Canada $17.95 plus taxes
- New Zealand $19.95
- United Kingdom £7.99
- United States $11.95 plus taxes

Order form

What books would you like?

A new-release book every three months The books are sent out in March, June, September and December. You will receive your first book in the appropriate month after we receive your order.	Quantity	Total
Option 1: two books over six months	2	
Option 2: four books over one year	4	
Option 3: eight books over two years	8	
Existing books in the series		
Animals are SMARTER than JACK (2005) *Canada and the USA only*		
Cats are SMARTER than JACK (2005)		
Dogs are SMARTER than JACK (2005)		
Australian animals are SMARTER than JACK 1 (2003) *Australia only*		
Australian animals are SMARTER than JACK 2 (2004) *Australia only*		
Canadian animals are SMARTER than JACK 1 (2004) *Canada only*		
Why animals are SMARTER than US (2004) *Australia, New Zealand, Canada and the USA only*		
Applicable taxes		
Subtotal for order		
Packaging and post: for orders of existing books only, please add $5 or £2		
Total		

For Canada, United States and United Kingdom orders only – using the lists on the preceding pages, please indicate which animal welfare charity in your country you would like to benefit from your order:

____

Choose the payment method

There are two ways you can pay:

- By cheque/check/postal order made out to the organisation you are sending it to and posted, along with your completed order form, to one of the addresses listed or
- Fill in the credit card details below:

Card type: Visa/Mastercard

Card number: | | | | | | | | | | | | | | | | |

Name on card: ____________________ Expiry date: ________

Complete your details

Your name: ____________________
Street address: ____________________
City/town: ____________________
State: ____________________
Postcode: ____________________
Country: ____________________
Phone: ____________________
Email: ____________________

Send in your order

Post your order to your nearest participating animal welfare charity or Smarter than Jack Limited at one of the addresses listed on pages 148–150, according to which country you live in.

Please note that some of the books are only available in certain countries.